A CAPPELLA MUSIC

IN THE PUBLIC WORSHIP
OF THE CHURCH

Revised Edition

by

Everett Ferguson

Published By
BIBLICAL RESEARCH PRESS
774 East North 15th Street
Abilene, Texas
79601

A CAPPELLA MUSIC

IN THE PUBLIC WORSHIP

OF THE CHURCH

By Everett Ferguson

Revised Edition

Library of Congress Catalog Card No. 72-76963

PREFACE

During my graduate study days at Harvard I lived in the same dormitory with a Greek Orthodox student who was a graduate of the University of Athens and a candidate for an advanced degree at Harvard. I asked him if it was correct that the Greek Orthodox churches did not use instrumental music in their public worship. He said, "Yes." Then I inquired as to the reasons why. His reply was most interesting to me: "We do not use instrumental music because it is not in the New Testament and it is contrary to the nature of Christian worship." By this he stated my case exactly for unaccompanied church music.

In elaborating the reasons for advocating *a capella* music in the public worship of the church I would like to apply a method of approach which I have found helpful in considering disputed matters of Christian practice. This methodology involves three steps: (1) an analysis of the New Testament evidence, (2) a testing of one's interpretation of the New Testament by the testimony of church history, and (3) a consideration whether there are doctrinal or theological reasons which explain or give meaning to the Biblical and historical evidence.

iii

CONTENTS

Page

PREFACE . . . .

Chapter

I. THE NEW TESTAMENT EVIDENCE 1
  A. Psallō: Its History and Meanings 1
  . The Linguistic Problem 1
  . Psallō in the Greek Old Testament 4
  . Dead Sea Scrolls 7
  . Greek Apocrypha and Pseudepigrapha 9
  . Josephus and Philo 11
  . Psallō in the New Testament 14
  . Psallō in Early Church Literature 18
  . Questions for Study 28
  B. The Context of New Testament Times 29

  . Temple Worship 29
  . Synagogue Worship 32
  . Philo on Music 37
  . Questions for Study 43

II. THE TESTIMONY OF HISTORY 47

  . Singing in Christian Worship 47
  . The Non-Use of an Instrument 52
  . Allegorical Interpretations of the Psalms 56
  . Statements Favorable to Instruments 64
  . Interpretations of the Word "Psalm" 68
  . Condemnations of Instrumental Music 74
  . The Significance of Culture 78
  . Later History 81
  . Questions for Study 84

III. DOCTRINAL CONSIDERATIONS 87

  . Nature of Worship 87
  . Spiritual Worship 88
  . Edification 90
  . The Classical Form of Church Music 91
  . Conclusion 94
  . Questions for Study 95

. Authors and Works Cited 96

. Glossary 98

THE NEW

TESTAMENT

Chapter I

THE NEW TESTAMENT EVIDENCE

According to the New Testament evidence instrumental music was not present in the worship of the early church. Singing incontestably was present in the corporate life of the early Christians (1 Corinthians 14:15, 26; Colossians 3:15 ff.; Ephesians 5:18ff.), and this was rooted in the practice of Jesus with his disciples (Mark 14:26). But there is no clear reference to instrumental music in Christian worship in any New Testament text.

PSALLŌ: ITS HISTORY AND MEANINGS

The Linguistic Problem

In order to support this conclusion about instrumental music's absence from early Christian worship some consideration must be given to the linguistic evidence. The main controversy has in the past concerned the Greek word *psallō*, which in the history of its usage has referred to both instrumental and vocal music. Consequently, it would seem, no one has been able to establish with finality that the word necessarily includes or excludes instrumental music. From an earlier classical (500-300 B.C.) meaning "to play," the word came to mean in Byzantine (300-500 A.D.) and modern Greek "to sing" or "to chant."[1] This transition in meaning was apparently effected by Jewish and early Christian usage. The real question is how the word is used in the specific New

[1] The evidence is in the standard lexicons. See now G. W. H. Lampe, *A Patristic Greek Lexicon* (Oxford: Clarendon Press, 1968), pp. 1539f. and G. Delling, "Hymnos" *et al., Theologisches Woerterbuch zum Neuen Testament*, Vol. 8 (Stuttgart: W. Kohlhammer, 1969), pp. 492-506. Cf. also Delling's comments in his *Early Christian Worship* (London: Darton, Longman, and Todd, 1962), pp. 85 ff. and W. S. Smith, *Musical Aspects of the New Testament* (Amsterdam, 1962), p. 47.

Testament texts (Rom. 15:9; 1 Cor. 14:15; Eph. 5:19; Jas. 5:13). Personally, I am convinced that later ecclesiastical usage and Jewish usage before and contemporary with the New Testament confirm a reference to vocal music exclusively in the New Testament texts. This is substantiated by the failure of the great majority of translators, lexicographers, commentators, and historians of church music to find a clear reference to instrumental music in the church's worship in any New Testament text. Nevertheless, since there is still controversy and misunderstanding, there is need to set forth clearly the evidence upon which decisions may be reached.

The root meaning of *psallō*, as defined by Liddell and Scott, is "pluck," and so most frequently "to play a stringed instrument."[2] In this limited sense the word referred to playing an instrument plucked with the fingers. In a broader sense the word could be used of making music in other ways. This was the meaning of the word in classical Greek. The Greek language has other words for "to play on an instrument," such as *kitharizō* ("to play the kithara," a zither or harp[3]) and *auleo* ("to play the aulos," or pipe) in 1 Corinthians 14.7, and *kreko* ("play"). Words meaning just "to sing" were *ado* (compare the noun "ode" and *humneo* ("to hymn" or "to praise")

On the other hand, E. A. Sophocles' *Greek Lexicon of the Roman and Byzantine Periods (From B.C. 146 to A.D. 1100)* defines *psallō* as *"chant, sing* religious hymns." The word thus later completely lost any connotation of an instrument and so in modern Greek (shaped by ecclesiastical usage) means simply "to sing." The problem is to determine at what period and among which peoples the word underwent its change.

---

[2] *A Greek-English Lexicon*, New Edition by H. S. Jones (Oxford: Clarendon Press), p. 2018.

[3] Since the names of modern instruments are often misleading, I shall normally transliterate the Greek words and at first occurrence give the usual English equivalent. Translations are my own except where noted otherwise.

Before considering this question we may note the parallel development in Latin. Latin borrowed the Greek word, and *psallere* is used by classical Latin authors in the sense of "play upon a stringed instrument" or "sing to the cithara."[4] Under the influence of church practice ecclesiastical Latin used the word with the meaning "chant (the Davidic psalms)"—this is normal from the Old Latin translation of the Bible and Tertullian's time (end of the second century) onward.[5] Tertullian uses the word in *On Fasting* 13:7 with the meaning "sing a psalm," with reference to a quotation from Ps. 133:1. This is the same usage which we shall find common in Greek church writers. He uses *psalmus* of the Old Testament Psalms, or occasionally a "song" (*The Flesh of Christ* 17.1 and *Against Marcion* V.8.12).

The Greek noun *psalmos* had a similar shift in meaning. From the sound made by playing on a *kithara* or a lyre it came to refer to the song sung to the instrument. In Jewish and Christian usage the word referred specifically (but not exclusively) to the Psalms of the Old Testament, thus to the words instead of the melody. A comparable shift may be seen in the English word *lyrics*—etymologically it is derived from the instrument "lyre" but now refers to the words of a song.

The classical meaning of *psallō* continued into Hellenistic and post-New Testament times. The satirist Lucian of Samosata in the second century A.D. said "It is impossible to pipe [*aulein*] without a pipe or to strum [*psallein*] without a lyre or to ride without a horse" (*Parasite* 17).[6] Aristides, the second century orator, could say "as easy as plucking [*pseleie*] a lyre's string" (*Orations* 26[14].31). The third (?) century treatise *De musica* by Aristides Quintilianus contains the statement, "If we wish to play (*psallein*), stretching the string in accord with the musical intervals which through the

---

[4] C. T. Lewis and Charles Short, *A Latin Dictionary* (Oxford: Clarendon Press), p. 1483. Passages illustrating this usage from the period of the first century B.C. to the second century A.D. are Sallust, *Catiline* xxv.2; Horace, *Odes* IV.xiii.7; *Epistles*, II.i.33; Suetonius, *Titus* 3; Aulus Gellius, *Attic Nights* XIX.ix.3.

[5] Alexander Souter, *A Glossary of Later Latin* (Oxford: Clarendon Press, 1957), p. 331.

[6] Translation by A. M. Harmon in Loeb Classical Library.

4

prescribed ratios will permit all the meters, some of our sounds will be found to have harmony and some to be discordant" (II. ii).[7]

Conversely, *psallō* with the simple meaning "sing" or "sing praise" ("sing the psalms") is well attested before New Testament times. Such is the usage of the *Psalms of Solomon*, Jewish hymns from the first century B.C. usually ascribed to the Pharisees but thoroughly representative of Palestinian religious piety shortly before the time of the New Testament. "Why do you sleep, my soul, and not bless the Lord? Sing (*psalle*) a new hymn to the God who is worthy to be praised. Sing (*psalle*) and be wakeful against his awakening, for good is a psalm to God from a good heart" (*Psalms of Solomon* 3:1, 2). The preference for vocal music may be seen in Psalm 15:3 from the same collection: "A new psalm with an ode in gladness of heart, the fruit of lips with the well-tuned instrument of the tongue, the first fruit of the lips from a pious and righteous heart." The similarity to Hebrews 13:15 may be noted. Also the wording in these verses shows the interchangeability of the words psalm, hymn, and ode (song). This coincides with the headings to the songs in this collection, which are variously titled psalm, hymn, or (in 17) also ode with no discernible distinction in meaning.[8]

Psallō in the Greek Old Testament

The use of *psallō* in the Septuagint, the Greek translation of the Old Testament begun in the third century B.C., has occupied an important place in the study of the word's history.[9] Where *psallō* translates the Hebrew word *nagan*, it refers to instrumental music. This is clear in 1 Samuel 16:16-18, 23; 18:10; 19:9 where there is reference to the instrument in the context. It is not so clear, but probable,

[7]Other passages usually cited include Plutarch, *Lives, Pericles* I.5 and Athenaeus, *Deipnosophists* 4. 183d.

[8]See further on this point pp. 14, 15.

[9]The Septuagint evidence is conveniently tabulated in the *Restoration Quarterly*, Volume 6, Number 2, pp. 57-66. I shall give Old Testament references according to the chapter and verse numbers in the English versions, which differs (especially in the Psalms) from the numbering in the Septuagint.

that the translator understood "playing" where the instrument is not mentioned (2 Kings 3:15; Ps. 33:3; 68:25).

Psallō occurs most frequently in the Septuagint as a translation of *zamar*, a Hebrew word with a similar etymology and development to its Greek translation. It is defined as "make music in praise of God," and the lexicon cites many instances "of singing," in a few of which instrumental accompaniment is mentioned in the context (but not included in the word itself), and several instances "of playing musical instruments."[10] In a few instances where *psallō* translates *zamar*, the mention of an instrument with the word shows that the idea is "to play" (Ps. 33:2; 71:22; 98:5; 144:9; 147:7; 149:3). Each of these references is cited by Brown, Driver, and Briggs for "making melody on an instrument" as a definition of *zamar*. The Greek construction in each instance is *psallō* followed by the preposition *en* ("with" or "on") and the name of the instrument.[11] Where the Lord is mentioned as the one to whom the music is directed, his name is in the dative case without a preposition. This construction will be of importance for Ephesians 5:19. In some instances instrumental accompaniment is present in the context, but it cannot be shown whether *psallo* means "play," or "sing" with an accompaniment also present (Ps. 57:7, 9, but see verse 8; 92:1 and see verse 3; 108:1, cf. verse 2), although translators have preferred the latter.

The context makes clear in several passages that only vocal praise is intended by the word *psallō*. Thus Psalms 47:6, 7 concludes in the Septuagint, "Sing [*psalate*] intelligibly." Psalms 71:23ff., "My lips will rejoice when I sing (*psalō*) to you ... and my tongue will be concerned with your righteousness all day." Psalms 105:2, "Sing to him and make melody (*psalate*) to him; narrate all his marvels." A large number of the occurrences of *psallō* in the Psalms are in

---

[10] Francis Brown, S. R. Driver, and Charles A. Briggs, *A Hebrew and English Lexicon of the Old Testament* (Oxford: Clarendon Press, 1955), p. 274.

[11] J. W. Roberts, "Psallō—Its Meaning: A Review," *Firm Foundation* March 24, April 7, May 12, June 9, 1959, makes the argument that *psallo* means "play" in the Septuagint only where this construction occurs or where the instrument is implied in the context. Certainly only in such instances can instrumental music be proved.

passages where the parallelism characteristic of Hebrew poetry is employed. In nearly every case the Septuagint translators have paired *psallō* with a word for vocal praise. Note the following instances: Psalms 18:49 (quoted in Rom. 15:9), "I will confess you among the nations, O Lord; and I will sing *(psalō)* to your name." Psalms 30:4, "Sing *(psalate)* to the Lord, O you his saints, in recollection of his holiness." Psalms 138:1, "I will confess you, Lord, with my whole heart, because you have heard the words of my mouth; and I will sing *(psalō)* to you before the angels." Psalms 135:3, "Praise the Lord, because he is good; sing *(psalete)* to his name, because he is good." Psalms 146:2, "I will praise the Lord in my life; I will sing *(psalō)* to my God as long as I live."

The word most often joined with *psallō* is *adō*, "sing"— Judges 5:3; Psalms 13:6; 21:13; 27:6; 57:7; 59:16ff.; 68:4, 32; 101:1; 104:33. One may note that in Psalms 13:6 *psallō* translates *shir*, which never meant anything but "sing" in the Hebrew. This frequent combination of *psallō* and *adō* in the Greek Old Testament probably accounts for Paul's usage of the two words together in Ephesians 5:19.

Only in Psalms 33:3; 98:4ff.; 144:9; and 149:3 do we have *psallō* with an instrument in parallelism with "singing."

Unless one is prepared to insist that in each instance of parallelism *psallō* is meant to add a new idea of playing, surely it is most natural to take these parallel expressions as synonymous statements. It is normal in Hebrew poetry to express the same idea in similar but different words. The Hebrew word in these verses is defined as "sing" or "sing praise," and we can assume that the Greek translators understood the Hebrew and sought to convey the same idea by *psallō*. Thus modern translators too have rendered "sing" or "make melody." Other occurrences of *psallō* in the Septuagint, all once more apparently meant to express singing in praise to God as *zamar* did, are Psalms 7:17; 9:2; 9:11; 30:12; 61:8; 66:2; 66:4; 68:33; 75:9; 98:4; 108:3. The reader may note the renderings of these verses in the Revised Standard Version ("sing" or "sing praises") and the New English Bible ("sing psalms").

If the precise meaning of certain verses may be in doubt, what is clear is that an instrument *did not inhere* in the word *psallō* in the Septuagint. *Psallō* could translate a word meaning "play" (*nagan*), a word meaning only "sing" (*shir*), or a general word (*zamar*). The meaning which would cover all occurrences is "make melody." This could include making melody on an instrument, as in the classical use of the word, but in the preponderance of occurrences it clearly refers to making melody with the voice.

Dead Sea Scrolls

The usage of *zamar*, the word which lies behind most of the occurrences of *psallō* in the Septuagint, on the threshold of New Testament times may be seen in the Dead Sea Scrolls. These documents from the Qumran community, which lived near the northwest shore of the Dead Sea, give us new information about Judaism in Palestine and contemporary with the New Testament. Unfortunately, this new source material has thus far not revealed a great deal about the worship practices of the Qumran community.

The Hebrew word *zamar* maintains its general meaning of "make melody," so that the context must indicate whether the melody is made on an instrument ("play") or with the voice ("sing"). *Zamar* means "sing" once and "play" the second time in one column of the Thanksgiving Scroll (*Hodayoth*), although from two different hymns:

> And into my mouth Thou hast put songs of thanksgiving and on my tongue a song of praise,
> and Thou hast circumcised my lips in the abode of rejoicing that I should sing [*zamar*] Thy favours
> and meditate on Thy power all the day long. (1 QH xi.4, 5)

> Therefore I will sing [or better play—*zamar*] upon the harp of deliverance
> upon the lyre of joy and the lute of gladness
> and upon the flute of praise without ceasing. (1 QH xi.23)[12]

---

[12] A. Dupont-Sommer, *The Essene Writings from Qumran* (Cleveland: World Publishing Co., 1962), pp. 236, 238.

In justification of Dupont-Sommer's preference for "sing" even in the latter passage may be noted the preference of the Scrolls for vocal music, as in the Manual of Discipline (Scroll of the Rule):

> With the offering of the lips will I bless Him
> . . . .
>
> I will sing [*zamar*] in Knowledge,
> and my whole lyre shall throb to the Glory of God,
> and my lute and harp to the holy Order which He has made.
> I will raise the flute of my lips because of His righteous measuring-cord.(1 QS x.6, 9)[13]

Comparison may be made to 1 Corinthians 14:15 and Hebrews 13:15 as well as to 1 QS ix.4, 5 where the sacrifice of lips replaces animal sacrifice. It seems clear that the instruments in the last quoted passage are metaphorical for the human body. This opens the way for understanding the instruments in the second citation from the Thanksgiving Scroll as also metaphorical (as presumably Dupont-Sommer did). Eric Werner has suggested that the Scrolls (aside from the War Scroll with its reference to many Old Testament instruments) may make only a metaphorical reference to instruments.[14] At any rate the present passage shows that the language of an instrument in reference to the human body to be found in Philo and the church fathers (see further below) was already present in Palestinian Judaism.

A large number of Hymns (the *Hodayoth*) are included in the Dead Sea Scrolls, but we lack information on their use, presumably they were for public performance,[15] but the manner of their rendition and whether accompanied is not indicated. If the group is related, as is commonly assumed, to the Therapeutae in Egypt, then we know something of the manner of the singing from the account of Philo which will be cited later.

---

[13] *Ibid.*, pp. 97, 98.

[14] Eric Werner, "Musical Aspects of the Dead Sea Scrolls," *Musical Quarterly* 43 (1957), pp. 21-37. Werner notes that the absence of instrumental music from Qumran would fit the ascetic piety of the group and their abstention from animal sacrifice, and he compares Paul and Philo.

[15] Svend Holm-Nielsen, *Hodayot: Psalms from Qumran* in *Acta Theologica Danica*, Vol. II (Aarhus, 1960), pp. 332-348.

Most occurrences of *psallō* and its compounds in Jewish apocryphal and intertestamental works are not completely unambiguous in their meaning. The little known *Testament of Job*, chapter 14, has a significant passage. It well illustrates the ambiguity possible in the words *psalmos* (psalm tune or psalm), *psalterion* (an instrument, but used by ecclesiastical writers for the book of Psalms), and *psallō*.

> I had six Psalms [or Psalm tunes] and a ten stringed kithara. I was accustomed to rouse myself daily after the widows were fed, and I took my kithara and played [or sang, *epsallon*] to them as they sang hymns. And I reminded them of God by the psaltery [or from the Book of Psalms] in order that they might glorify the Lord. And if my handmaids were still murmuring among themselves, I took up again my stringed instrument and I sang to them [praised, *epsallon*] the wages of reward and caused them to cease from their negligent murmuring.[16]

If we had only the first statement in which *psallō* occurs, one would certainly translate "play": "I took up my kithara and played to them and they sang hymns." But the second occurrence of the word can only refer to a vocal expression. One does not "play" the "wages of reward." Unless the author has used the word in two different senses so close together, then we should translate "sing" at the first occurrence also. "Job" was playing his kithara, but he was singing too, for the situation described is responsorial singing with the widows singing the refrain of the psalms. The usage may be the intermediate meaning "sing to accompaniment." The instrumental accompaniment is certainly present in the context, but there is still a real question whether the instrument inheres in the word *psallō* in this document. Such may be the case. But it is also possible that we have only the meaning "sing." Lest the evidence seem to be pushed too far, it is perhaps best to see the meaning "make melody," which

---

[16]The date of the work is debated and the text is unsettled. I have translated from *Testamentum Iobi*, ed. S. P. Brock, in *Pseudepigrapha Veteris Testamenti Graece*, ed. A. M. Denis, Vol. II (Leiden: Brill, 1967).

could be applied to either instrumental (the first) or vocal (the second) music.

Modern translators and students of the better known intertestamental works generally see a reference to vocal music only in the usage of *psallō* and its cognates. Thus the Revised Standard Version and the New English Bible uniformly render the references to *hieropsaltai* in 1 Esdras (1:15; 5:27; 8:22; 9:24) as "temple singers." 2 Maccabees 1 quotes an account of the reinstitution of sacrifice under Nehemiah following the exile. While the sacrifice was being consumed, the priests led the people in responsorial prayers. Verse 30 then reads: "The priests sang [*epepsallon*] the hymns" [*hymnous*]. The object seems to certify the vocal translation of *epipsallō* in this passage.

Sirach (Ecclesiasticus) 9:4's *psallousa* is translated in the Revised Standard Version "woman singer." Sirach 47:8-10 is an important passage. In detailing the achievements of David, who in the Old Testament introduced instrumental music into the cult, the author makes reference only to his vocal contributions:

> In all that he did he gave praise to the Holy One, the Most High, with words of glory; with his whole heart he hymned and loved his Maker. He placed singers (*psaltōdous*) before the altar to make sweet melody with their voices [*ēchous*, a word primarily, although not exclusively, for vocal sounds] .... They praised his holy name, and the sanctuary resounded [*ēchein*] from early morning.

Psaltōdoi is apparently the correct reading also in Sirach 50:18, part of a passage fully quoted later on the Temple worship. Instrumental music is in the context, but *psaltōdoi* refers only to the musicians who sang, as the verse makes clear: "The singers [*psaltōdoi*] praised with their voices; they made sweet melody with rich sound" [*ēchō* again].

Hymns and songs are several times mentioned in the Apocrypha as part of Jewish religious life, and not uncommonly with instrumental accompaniment but without the use of *psallō* or its cognates. Accordingly, in Judith 16:1, 2, 13 we read:

Then Judith began this thanksgiving with all
Israel, and all the people loudly sang this song of
praise. And Judith said, "Begin a song to my God
with tambourines, sing to my Lord with cymbals.
Raise to him a new psalm and give praise; exalt him
and call upon his name . . . . I will hymn to my God a
new hymn."

Sirach 39:14, 15 says, "Scatter the fragrance and praise him
with song . . . magnify his name and acknowledge him with
praise, with songs of the lips and with lyres, and so shall you
speak in praise."

On the other hand, there was being expressed the view
that the tongue was better than an instrument: "The *aulos*
and the *psaltērion* make pleasant melody, but the tongue is
more pleasing than both" (Sirach 40:21 cf. 51:1, 10 for vocal
praise). Therefore, we are prepared for the preference for the
vocal use of *psallō* in Jewish religious literature which we
have found exemplified in the *Psalms of Solomon*. Nevertheless, Hellenistic Jews writing for Gentile audiences kept to
the classical meaning of *psallō*.

Josephus and Philo

Josephus, the Jewish historian, is strictly classical in his
use of *psallō*. David is described in *Antiquities* VI.viii.167,
following the Septuagint, as one who "knew to play the
zither [*pasllein*] and to sing [*adein*] hymns." Section 168
describes him as "both speaking hymns and playing [*psallōn*]
on the kinura." Compare VII.xii.305 where David composed
hymns and odes to God, made instruments, and taught the
Levites to "hymn" God on them. *Antiquities* IX.xiii.269
speaks of a sacrifice under Hezekiah: while the priests offered
sacrifice, "the Levites standing around in a circle with their
musical instruments sang [*ēdon*] hymns to God and played
their harps [*epsallon*] as they were taught by David, and the
remaining priests who had trumpets sounded them with those
who sang." *Antiquities* XI.iii.67 refers to "playing harps
[*psallomenoi*] and flutes and clashing cymbals." *Antiquities*
XII.viii.349 has "playing harps [*psallontes*] and singing
hymns [*hymnountes*]."

Josephus uses *psalmos* in its etymological sense of the tune played (the "plucking") on a stringed instrument. Thus in *Antiquities* IX.iii.35 the context requires that *psallein* is "to play the harp" and *psalmos* (if it is the correct reading rather than *psallonta*) is the "sound of the harp." *Antiquities* VI.xi.214 is "to sing away the spell with the sound of the harp (*psalmo*) and hymns." *Antiquities* XII.vii.323 has the same combination of words, "honoring God with hymns and playing of harps" (*psalmois*). It might be argued that some of the above could be rendered "psalms" or "songs of praise" (which is clearly correct for *psalmos* in most cases in late Jewish and Christian literature), but the association in *Antiquities* VII.iv.80 makes the instrumental meaning definite: "hymning God and singing every kind of native melody with the mingled sounds of stringed instruments, and dancing, and tunes of the harp (*psalmōn*), as well as trumpet and cymbals."

The classical use of the *psallō* family of words in Josephus is normative and need not be demonstrated further from the context and sources of Josephus. In many of these passages Josephus has introduced *psallō* or *psalmos* where it is not in his sources and his departure in terminology from his Biblical and intertestamental sources is to be noted. As one example, in *Antiquities* XII.vii.323 above Josephus has found a reference to harps in the account he is following (1 Maccabees 4:54), and he has substituted a reference to the sound made by the harp (*psalmos*). It is characteristic that Josephus refers to the Old Testament Psalms not as *psalmoi* but as *humnoi* (cf. *Against Apion* I.40). Josephus' departures from normal Jewish word usage is to be explained by the Gentile audience for which he is writing.

Philo of Alexandria, a Jewish philosophical writer, too always refers to the Psalms as "hymns," "hymnody," or "songs" (*asma*)—e.g., *Migration of Abraham* 157; *Contemplative Life* 25; and uniformly in the introduction of his Psalm quotations. Philo has a great deal to say about music, especially vocal music, and this must be examined in due course, but the index to his works does not show the word *psallō*. The cognate *epipsallō* is used with the meaning "play by hand," but in a metaphorical sense. The soul of the wise man is played harmoniously like a lyre (*On the Unchange-*

ableness of God 24). The same metaphorical meaning of "play" on an instrument lies behind *On Dreams* I.37 where the heavens are considered musical instruments "in order that the hymns which are sung in honor of the Father of the universe may be accompanied [*epipsallōntai*] musically." Section 35 elaborates the thought: man's mind is capable of offering God hymns, praise, and blessings; this vocal expression receives its instrumental accompaniment in the harmonious movement of the heavenly bodies. These thoughts are typical of Philo's emphasis on rational praise and his allegorical interpretation of instrumental music (either the soul or the heavens).

In view of Philo's rich musical terminology the absence of *psallō* from his extensive body of writings calls for an explanation. A plausible hypothesis would be that Philo is aware of the primarily instrumental connotation of the word to pagan readers. Philo's own emphasis is on a different kind of music (as will appear later), and so he avoids a word which might be misleading. It is disputed whether Philo was writing primarily for Gentiles or for his own people, but he was certainly conscious of Greek connotations. *Psallō* was being used in an accomodative sense by Jews for their own kind of sacred music. Philo prefers words which were not ambiguous. A parallel is to be found in his preference of *humnos* for *psalmos*. For a modern reader and for his fellow Jews there would have been no doubt that *psalmos* meant psalm, but since the classical meaning was "the tune played," Philo chose a term that unambiguously meant the verbal content. Behind the words *humnos* or *asma* is sometimes clearly the word *psalmos*. I would suppose that in a similar way behind at least some of Philo's use of the verbs *adō* and *humneō* are to be found in popular Jewish speech *psallō*. Thus evidence which might seem negative to the line of development being traced actually turns out to support it.

Regardless of the conclusion to be drawn from Philo's silence, linguistic evidence would seem to indicate that it was in Jewish religious language that we find the shift in usage for *psallō* from instrumental to vocal music (Septuagint, *Psalms of Solomon*, etc.). Where the instrumental idea was present, it was treated metaphorically (Philo, perhaps the Dead Sea Scrolls). This linguistic development will be seen to correspond to the developments in regard to the music of Jewish worship, which will furnish a further clarification of the background to worship in the early church. Before pursuing that subject we may continue the linguistic history and look at the New Testament passages employing *psallō* and apply the insights gained from Jewish Greek literature to their interpretation.

Psallō *in the New Testament*

Psallo is a principal word for "sing" in the New Testament. *Adō* occurs only twice (Colossians 3:16; Ephesians 5:19), and *humneō* apart from an Old Testament quotation (Hebrews 2:12) occurs only in the Synoptic Gospels (Matthew 26:30; Mark 14:26) and in Acts 16:25. *Psallō* occurs in an Old Testament quotation in Romans 15:9; in James 5:13; in 1 Corinthians 14:15; and Ephesians 5:19. The quotation from Psalms 18:49 was considered above in the classification of passages from the Septuagint. The context and the parallelism with praying make the translation "sing" certain in James and 1 Corinthians. The whole discussion in 1 Corinthians 14 has to do with what was spoken (note especially verses 19 and 26). No serious effort has been made to read "play" in these passages. Only the translation of Ephesians 5:19 has been contested, and indeed unless there is a reference to the instrument in this verse, it is impossible to find an explicit reference to instrumental music in Christian worship in the New Testament.

The parallel to Ephesians 5:19 in Colossians 3:16 mentions "teaching, admonishing, . . . and singing" (*adō*)—all vocal activities. Sometimes an effort is made to find an instrument in the word *psalmos* (psalm). Although the word originally signified what was played on a lyre and then sung to the accompaniment of a lyre (see above), it was commonly used by the time of the Christian era among Jews and then Christians for the Old Testament Psalms or compositions of a similar type. Words written to be accompanied can be sung without accompaniment, and singing is all that is said about the psalms here. Indeed during the New Testament era the terms psalm, hymn, and ode were being used without any precise distinction, despite their different etymological histories. Passages cited thus far in this study provide part of the evidence for this conclusion, and such is commonly held by contemporary scholars.[17] A parallel from early church literature is the Pseudo Justin, *Epistle to Zeno and Serenus* 9, which counsels against much speaking and cites as the kinds of words which may be spoken "hymns, psalms, odes, and verbal praise."

Ephesians 5:19 adds "making melody" (*psallontes*) to the "singing" of the Colossians passage. The joining of *psallō* and *adō* as parallel expressions for verbal praise in the Greek translation of the Psalms suggests that this is the meaning here. If it is contended that *psallō* supplies the instrumental accompaniment to the singing and "in your heart" should be rendered "heartily," then the following response may be offered. It is true that the prepositional phrase "in the heart" can be rendered adverbially as "heartily," but in this instance the pronoun "your" is left dangling with an unlikely possibility of being construed with Lord. The patristic interpretation saw the phrase as referring to the mental understanding accompanying the pronouncing of the words. For instance, Chrysostom says in *Homily* XIX, *On Ephesians* V, 19:

> Learn to sing psalms [*psallein*), and you will see the pleasure of the activity. For those who sing psalms [*psallontes*] are filled with the Holy Spirit, even as those singing satanic odes are filled with an unclean spirit. What is "in your hearts to the Lord"? It means giving attention with understanding. For those who do not pay attention merely sing [*psallousi*], sounding the words while their heart roams elsewhere. (PG 62:129)

---

[17]W. S. Smith, *Musical Aspects of the New Testament* (Amsterdam, 1962), pp. 61ff.; Théodore Gérold, *Les pères de l'église et la musique* (Paris, 1931), pp. 116f.; cf. Oskar Soehngen,"Theologische Grundlagen der Kirchenmusik," *Leiturgia* IV (1961), p. 8, who adds that in the New Testament references *psallō* has lost reference to the instrument and can be translated "praise," certainly not "play," as Luther and Dibelius do (p. 12).

The same interpretation of the passage is given in his *Exposition on Psalm* XLI, 1:

> What is "in your hearts"? He says "with understanding," lest the tongue speak words while the mind spends its time wandering about everywhere else. (PG 55:157)

Chrysostom's *Homily* IX, *On Colossians* III, 2 is similar:

> Not merely with the mouth but with attention. For the latter is to sing to God, but the former is to sing to the air, for the voice is merely dispersed. (PG 62:364)

Finally, Chrysostom comments on *psallō* with the "spirit and understanding" of 1 Corinthians 14:15: "In order that the tongue may speak and the mind be not ignorant of the words spoken" (*Homily* XXXV, *On 1 Corinthians* 14:15 in PG 61:300). Theodoret's *Interpretation of Ephesians* V, 19 says, "He sings [*psallei*] in heart who not only moves the tongue but also excites the mind to the understanding of the words spoken" (PG 82:545 C).

Even more decisive for the meaning of Ephesians 5:19 are the Old Testament parallels: *psallō en* plus an instrument in certain passages in the Psalms (1 Sam. 16:16; Ps. 33:2; 71:22; 98:5; 144:9; 147:7; 149:3) meant to make melody "on the instrument named" to the Lord. According to these parallels, if Paul has thought of *psallō* in the broader sense of "make melody" or even "play," then he has specified the instrument on which the melody is to be made, namely the heart. These Old Testament parallels would also rule out the possibility of construing "in your hearts" with "sing" as well as with "make melody."

Paul's "singing, and making melody" is likely to be understood as simply giving a very full statement without any precise distinctions. (For such double expressions in Ephesians compare 1:1, 9, 12 and frequently.) Certainly it is hard, apart from arbitrary assumptions about the use of *psallō*, to find any clear distinction between *adō* and *psallō* as used in many Old Testament passages where they occur together. There is also an early post-Pauline reference in

Christian literature where the two words are synonyms: Justin Martyr, *Dialogue with Trypho* 74:3,

> He bids those of all the earth who know this saving mystery, namely the suffering of Christ by which he saved them, to sing and praise [*psallontas,* "make melody"] the God and Father of the universe.

The vocal use of *psallō* by this second century author is confirmed by 29:2,

> For these words have not been fashioned by me nor adorned with human skill, but David sang [*epsallen,* or "sang them in the psalms"] them, Isaiah preached them, Zachariah proclaimed them, and Moses wrote them.

So, no instrument is found in the New Testament reference, but only vocal praise, and thus no New Testament authority for instrumental music in worship is available.

Since Paul has been discussing ethical conduct in the context of Ephesians 5:19 and Colossians 3:16, some have questioned whether these verses apply to the assembly of the church. The personal relationships involved in both letters are clearly based on what is appropriate to membership in the church (Ephesians 4:25; Colossians 3:15). The corporate life of the church is the theme throughout Ephesians and certainly in chapters 4-6, the so-called practical section of the treatise. The corporate nature of what is described in Ephesians 5:19 is made explicit by the "one another" (cf. the same word in 4:32). Colossians adds that the "word of Christ" is to dwell "among you," "in your midst."[18] Moreover, Ephesians is making a contrast between pagan religious practices, where drunkenness and immorality were often associated with the cult, and Christian worship (verse 18). Both Colossians and Ephesians are describing a setting where the word of the Lord is dispensed and song to God is engaged in. Recent commentators and translators suggest that a break is to be made in Colossians 3:16 between the "teaching and admonishing one another in all wisdom" and

---

[18] Delling in *Theologisches Woerterbuch*, Vol. 8, p. 501.

the "singing psalms, hymns, and spiritual songs with grace in your hearts." So two activities are to characterize the abundant presence of the word of the Lord among Christians. The same may be true for Ephesians 5:19. The equivalent of the rich activity of the word indwelling the church in Colossians is the fulness of the Spirit in Ephesians. In any case it is not a private religious exercise which is described. The statements accord well with the description of a worship assembly in 1 Corinthians 14 where the activity of the Spirit results in various types of speaking, song, and prayer, and where the emphasis is on understandable verbal edification (done for one another). The assembly of the church is part of the Christian life, and indeed Paul sees it as important in counteracting the problems confronting these churches in Asia to whom the letters are sent. Thus he quite naturally includes reference to what was done in public worship in discussing the expressions of the corporate life of Christians in their relations one with another.

The history of *psallō's* usage indicates a purely vocal reference in the New Testament. To complete the philological history we now turn to the usage of *psallō* in early Christian authors.

Psallō *in Early Church Literature*

Clement of Alexandria (end of the second century) is the first Christian writer to employ an extensive musical vocabulary and so affords ample materials for word study, a task facilitated by an excellent index to the critical edition of his works. Although Clement was Hellenic in education, he completely represents the Judaeo-Christian usage of *psallō* and attitude toward instrumental music.

Clement's most common usage of *psallō* is to introduce quotations from the Psalms. We may translate, "The Holy Spirit (or David) sings . . . " or "says in the Psalms . . . ." Particularly clear is *Instructor* I,i,1,1, "Singing together [*sunadontes*] with the prophecy which sings" [*psallousē*], followed by Psalms 73:1. No less explicit of the vocal meaning is *Instructor* II.x.110,2: "This word sings [*psallē*] through David concerning our Lord, saying . . . ." The frequency of this usage speaks eloquently of the meaning the word had for Clement, for it is only the words of the Psalms

which the statements have in view: *Instructor* I.viii.73,1;
I.ix.88,3; II.iv.41,4; II.x.113,4; *Miscellanies* I.i.8,3;
III.iv.33,4; V.x.64,2; VI.viii.64,5; VI.xvi.145,3. This usage,
which coincides with Justin, *Dialogue with Trypho* 29:2,
cited on page 17, prepares us for the common ecclesiastical
meaning "to sing the Psalms."

Other passages are equally clear about a vocal meaning
for *psallō* in Clement of Alexandria. The question of "What is
the chorus which is singing?" (*psallon*, in view of the context
indefensibly rendered "play" in *Ante-Nicene Fathers*, Vol. 2,
p. 249) is answered by Psalms 146:1, 2 as the "congregation
praising" (*Instructor* II.iv.44,4). *Exhortation to the Heathen*
I.8,3 uses *psallō* equal to *adō*, because of the parallel drawn
between the physician who addresses some with the voice of
song (*adō*) and the Savior who cheers by the voice of song
(*psallō*). The company the word keeps is evident from
Miscellanies VI.xiv.113,3 (cited in full later), "praising,
hymning, blessing, singing [*psallousa*]." The hymn at the
close of the *Instructor* is introduced by the exhortation "Let
us sing" (*psalōmen*) followed by the words of the hymn. See
also *Instructor* III.xi.80,4 cited on page 50 in the descriptions
of the church's practice. Rarely is Clement's usage unclear (as
in *Miscellanies* I,i,16,1), and even where not conclusive
(Miscellanies VI.xi.89,4-90,1), the meaning seems to be vocal.
Epipsallo is used in the sense "make response" *(Miscellanies*
V.viii).

Because of the numerous parallel passages above about
David and the Psalms, we must say that "playing" in the
Ante-Nicene Fathers (vol. II, p. 500) translation of *Miscellanies* VI.xi.88,1 is incorrect. "David singing Psalms [*psallō*]
and prophesying . . . hymning God" would be more accurate
(Singing is put on the same plane with prophesying in the
Confession of Cyprian 17.) The classical meaning has
obtruded itself, inconsistently with Clement's established
usage, in the rendering of *Exhortation to the Heathen*
XII,119,2. More accurate (and more consistent with the
other phrases) would be "The chorus is the righteous, the
song [*asma*] is a hymn to the King of the universe; the
maidens sing [*psallousin*], the angels praise, the prophets
speak." A recollection of the Biblical narrative has influenced
the translator at *Exhortation to the Heathen* I.5,4 to say

David cured Saul "by merely playing," when the verb is *ado*, which always means "singing," and certainly should be so rendered here. Unless Clement has been careless or free here, the substitution of *ado* for the Septuagint's *psallo* would speak forcefully for Clement's understanding of the meaning of the word.

When Clement wants to say "sing and play," he uses *ado* and a word for playing on an instrument, such as *kitharizo* (*Exhortation to the Heathen* II.31,3), *phormizo* (IV.59,1), or he says "sing [*ado*] with the lyre [*kithara*]" (*Miscellanies* I.xvi.78,5).

Clement's fullest treatment of music comes in *Instructor* II.iv.42-44 in his discussion of proper conduct at banquets. In contrast to the sensuous music at pagan entertainments Clement quotes Psalms 150 and proceeds to give an allegorical interpretation:

> The Spirit, distinguishing from such revelry the divine service, sings, "Praise Him with the sound of the trumpet;" for with the sound of trumpet He shall raise the dead. "Praise Him on the psaltery;" for the tongue is the psaltery of the Lord. "And praise Him on the lyre." By the lyre is meant the mouth struck by the Spirit, as it were by a plectrum. "Praise with the timbrel and the dance," refers to the Church meditating on the resurrection of the dead in the resounding skin. "Praise Him on the chords and organ." Our body He calls an organ, and its nerves are the strings, by which it has received harmonious tension, and when struck by the Spirit, it gives forth human voices. "Praise Him on the clashing cymbals." He calls the tongue the cymbal of the mouth, which resounds with the pulsation of the lips. Therefore He cried to humanity, "Let every breath praise the Lord," because He cares for every breathing thing which He hath made. For man is truly a pacific instrument; while other instruments, if you investigate, you will find to be warlike, inflaming to lusts, or kindling up amours, or rousing wrath. (41, 4-42, 1)

He continues further:

> The one instrument of peace, the Word alone by which we honour God, is what we employ. We no longer employ the ancient psaltery, and trumpet, and timbrel, and flute, which those expert in war and

contemners of the fear of God were wont to make
use of also in the choruses at their festive assemblies;
that by such strains they might raise their dejected
minds. $(42, 3)$[19]

One may note later in the chapter the interpretation of
the ten-stringed psaltery as the Word Jesus $(43, 3)$.
This allegorical interpretation of the instruments in the Old
Testament as really the parts of the body was to have a great
vogue later in the church (see pp. 56ff.) Clement seems to
have taken his cue from Philo. As Philo, he compares man,
composed of body and soul and like a miniature universe, to
an instrument:

> The Word of God, despising the lyre and harp,
> which are but lifeless instruments, and having tuned
> the universe by the Holy Spirit, and especially man
> ... makes melody [*psallō*] to God on this instrument
> of many tones; and to this instrument—I mean
> man—he sings [*prosadō*] accordingly: "For thou art
> my harp, and pipe, and temple." (*Exhortation to the
> Heathen* I.5.3)

Clement is typical also in that where he appears to preserve
the classical meaning of *psallō*, he does so only in a
metaphorical sense. At another place Clement is explicit on
the allegorical interpretation which he gives to the instruments in the Psalms:

> The lyre, according to its primary signification,
> may by the psalmist be used figuratively for the Lord;
> according to its secondary, for those who continually
> strike the chords of their souls under the direction of
> the Choir-master, the Lord. And if the people saved
> be called the lyre, it will be understood to be in
> consequence of their giving glory musically, through
> the inspiration of the Word and the knowledge of
> God, being struck by the Word so as to produce faith.
> (*Miscellanies* VI.xi.88)[20]

---

[19]Quoted from the translation in the *Ante-Nicene Fathers*, Vol. II, pp. 248
and 249.

[20]Quotation from *Ante-Nicene Fathers*, Vol. II, p. 500.

Returning to the *Instructor* passage, we note that after citing Ephesians 5:19 Clement gives one of the rare approbations of an instrument to be found in the church fathers. "Even if you wish to sing [*adein*] and make melody [*psallein*] to [*pros*] the kithara or lyre, there is no blame" (*Instructor* II.iv.43,3). The two verbs, *adō* and *psallō*, are joined by *te kai* ("both ... and"), a construction which means that they must be construed in the same way. Whatever relation *adō* sustains to the instruments which are named, *psallō* does too. Clement uses later in the context (II.iv.44,3) the same construction as here, *adō pros* plus the name of an instrument (*lyran*, "lyre"), when he wants to say "sing to the accompaniment" of that instrument. The use of *pros* plus the accusative of an instrument is a recognized Greek phrase for "with the accompaniment of" a musical instrument.[21] Therefore, *psallō* cannot mean "play on" in this passage; to "play" to the accompaniment of an instrument is meaningless. Like *adō, psallō* is *what is done* "to the accompaniment of the kithara and lyre." We have then either the familiar combination "sing and make melody" without precise differentiation of meaning, or if a new idea is introduced by *psallō*, then we have "sing psalms" to the accompaniment of the kithara and lyre. The translation "sing psalms" fits Clement's usage elsewhere. And this may be the precise emphasis here—one can sing even psalms to an instrument at home. Later in the passage Clement uses *eulogein* (to bless) and *psallein* (to sing praises) together as equivalent (44, 1). He notes that "The apostle calls the psalm 'a spiritual song' " (44, 1). He continues that our songs at a banquet are to be "hymns to God" (44, 3).

This passage, therefore, proves to be no exception to Clement's normal use of *psallō* for vocal expressions. The qualified approval of the lyre and kithara (see the negative judgment earlier in the passage above) is in contrast to the condemnation of other instruments earlier in the context. Even so, Clement is talking about what is permitted at a banquet. He is not describing the worship assemblies of the church. Nor is he describing an *agapē*. Clement's discussion of the Christian love-feast comes elsewhere (*Instructor* II.i) and

---

[21] Liddell and Scott, *op. cit.,* p. 1498.

the present discussion of banquets is part of an extended cycle of activities in daily life. If some of his statements seem to refer to a religious context, this is because it is characteristic of Clement to weave together texts about religious worship with his discussion of daily activities. Other church writers will advocate substituting the psalms for licentious instrumental music in the home life of Christians (pp. 75, 76).

Greek Christian authors of the third century continue the vocal use of *psallō*. Origen in his treatise *On Prayer* 2, 4 uses the word in the sense "sing" (synonymously with *humneō*) with reference to 1 Corinthians 14:15.

> For neither can our understanding pray, unless previously the Spirit prays, hearkening as it were to it, nor likewise can it sing [*psalai*] and hymn the Father in Christ with rhythm, melody, measure and harmony, unless the Spirit . . . first praise and hymn him.[22]

The third century bishop of Olympus in Lycia, Methodius, knew his classics but used *psallō* in its ecclesiastical sense of "sing" without accompaniment. "Christ sings [*psallei*] these praises," he says of descriptions of virginity (*Banquet* VII.1). Just before the responsive hymn toward the end of the *Banquet* Methodius writes that Thecla "sang [*psallō*] melodiously," and what was sung is described as a "thanksgiving hymn" (XI.2). In the hymn itself "singing the new song" is expressed by *psallō*. Methodius in another work speaks of the martyrs singing [*psallō*] Psalms 124:2-7 (*On the Resurrection* I, 56, 4).

Eusebius at the beginning of the fourth century describes certain Egyptian martyrs of the Diocletian persecution:

> They received the final sentence of death with joy and laughter and gladness so that they sang

---

[22]Translation by J. E. L. Oulton in *Library of Christian Classics*, Vol. II (Philadelphia: Westminster, 1954), p. 242.

[*psallein*] and sent up hymns and thanksgiving to the God of the universe until they drew their last breath. (*Church History* VIII.ix.5) [23]

The vocal use of *psalmos* is evident when Eusebius speaks of Christians who had been banished to the mines returning home after the persecution: "Yea, thronging crowds of men went on their journey, praising God in the midst of thoroughfares and market-places with songs and psalms" (*ibid.* IX.1.11). Eusebius' earlier sources used the words in the same way. Concerning the heretical Paul of Samosata, for a time bishop of Antioch in the third century, Eusebius refers to his "training women to sing hymns" [*psalmodein*] to himself and then mentions those "who sing psalms [*psallontes*] to him and utter his praises in the congregation" (*ibid.* VII.xxx.10,11). Concerning more orthodox hymn writing, Eusebius quotes an anonymous second century author, "As many psalms and odes written by faithful brethren from the beginning hymn Christ as the Word of God and speak of him as a God" (*ibid.* V.xxviii.5-9). The hymning of Christ in psalms and odes shows the interchangeability of these words. Furthermore, this passage shows that "psalms" had been extended by early Christians from the Old Testament book to include their own compositions. (Cf. the use of *psalmodia* in VII.xxiv.4.) The word, as a result of being a designation for Old Testament hymns, had thus been transformed into purely vocal compositions. Such is the case here, for these psalms "hymn Christ" and "speak of him as God," and such was the regular Christian usage.

Athanasius, fourth century bishop of Alexandria, in his *Epistle to Marcellinus* repeatedly uses *psallō* in instructing which Psalm is to be sung on certain occasions. Similarly in his introduction to his Psalms commentary the author of a Psalm is said to *psallō* it, in parallel with statements for "saying" it (PG 27:57C). Note *Epistle to Marcellinus* 29:

Those who do not read (aloud) the sacred songs in this manner do not sing [*psallousi*] with under-

---

[23]This and the following quotation are from the translation in the Loeb Classical Library. Cf. Eusebius' *Commentary On Psalms* 65:10-15, cited on p. 51.

standing ... But those singing [*psallontes*] in the above described manner, so as to present the melody of the words from the rhythm of the soul and the harmony with the spirit, these sing [*psallousi*] with the tongue but make melody [*psallontes*] with the mind, and they profit greatly not only themselves but those who wish to hear them.

If the vocal use of *psallō* seems belabored, the references are being multiplied because of the claim that an instrument inhered in the word. Cyril of Jerusalem in the mid-fourth century shows the clearly vocal use of *psallō*.

And again, let the young women sit together in like manner, either singing [*psallōn*] or reading quietly, so that their lips speak, but others' ears do not hear the sound: "for I permit not a woman to speak in the church." (*Procatechesis* 14, PG 33:356B).

A parallel thought is expressed in the fifth century by Isidore of Pelusium, *Epistles* I.90 (PG 78:244D-245A). Basil of Caesarea in Cappadocia, *Homily on Psalm* 28, says:

You have a psalm, you have prophecy, evangelical commandments, the preaching of the apostles. Let the tongue sing (*psalletō*), let the mind interpret the meaning of the words, in order that you may sing with the spirit and sing with the mind also. (PG 29:304A)

The fourth-century *Apostolic Constitutions* reflects ecclesiastical usage.

If you stay at home, read the books of the Law, of the Kings, with the Prophets; sing [*psallō*] the hymns of David; and study diligently the Gospel. (I.v.2)[24]

The next chapter fixes the meaning of *psallō* here by its parallel, "If you desire something to sing [*asmatikōn*] you have the Psalms" (I.vi.5). The widow's conduct is to be "sitting at home, singing [*psallō*] and praying, and reading,

---

[24] The translations are adapted from the *Ante-Nicene Fathers*, Vol. VII.

and watching, and fasting; speaking to God continually in songs [*odē*] and hymns" (III.vii.7). Book VIII.xxxiv.10 states:

> If it is not possible to assemble either in the church or in a house, let every one by himself sing [*psallō*], and read, and pray, two or three together.

The descriptions of what was done in the assembly of the church correspond. On Sunday:

> But when there have been two lessons read, let some other person sing [*psallō*] the hymns of David, and let the people join in the singing [*hupopsallō*] at the conclusions of the verses. (II.lvii.6)

> O bishop, if you are speaking the word of God, or hearing him that sings [*ho psallōn*] or reads ... (III.viii.4).

With this compare VI.xxx.2, "reading the holy books and singing [*psallō*] for the martyrs." The one who leads the chanting of the psalms in the church is *ho psallōn* (VIII.xiv.1). At other times besides Sunday:

> But assemble yourselves together every day, morning and evening, singing psalms [*psallō*] and praying in the Lord's house. (II.lix.2)

The heavenly worship is described with the same word:

> The holy seraphim, together with the six-winged cherubim, who sing [*psallō*] to Thee their triumphal song, cry out with never-ceasing voices, "Holy, holy, holy ... (VII.xxxv.3)

> But Israel, your church on earth, taken out of the Gentiles, emulating the heavenly powers night and day, with a full heart and willing soul sings [*psallō*, and there follows a Psalm quotation]. (VII. xxxv.4)

As in the last example, Book V.xx.8 continues the usage familiar from Clement of Alexandria of introducing a Psalm quotation with *psallō*: "Him David knew, and sung [*psallō*] an ode concerning him." It should be evident that there is a consistent use of *psallō* in the *Apostolic Constitutions* to mean "to sing" or "to chant the Psalms." The compiler's vocal use is uniform.

By the end of the fourth century the ecclesiastical sense is so uniform as to need no further documentation. When further statements are introduced in the treatment of the historical evidence for the church's practice, note will be made of further occurrences of the word *psallō*. The only exceptions in ecclesiastical authors that I have noted are where the etymological meaning of the word is used metaphorically.

QUESTIONS FOR STUDY

1. What "conclusion" is stated at the beginning, to be supported later by the evidence?

2. Why is *psallō* of such importance in the study of church music? What is the etymology and classical usage of *psallō*? Is this meaning found later than New Testament times?

3. What evidence is there for the use of *psallō* in reference to *a cappella* singing before New Testament times?

4. Why and how does the meaning of words change?

5. What three Hebrew words does *psallō* translate in the Old Testament? What are their meanings?

6. How does Josephus use the word *psallō*? How do you account for the absence of the word in Philo? What are the dates of these men, and what is their importance for New Testament word usage?

7. Does an instrument inhere in the word *psallō* or must its presence be determined by the context? Is an instrument to be inferred from any New Testament passages using *psallō*?

8. What words are used in the New Testament for singing? In what passages do they occur?

9. Do Ephesians 5:19 and Colossians 3:16 refer to an assembly of the church or private religious activities? Give reasons for your answer.

10. How is *psallō* used by early Christian writers after the New Testament?

THE CONTEXT OF

NEW TESTAMENT TIMES

Temple Worship

The first instances of the purely vocal use of *psallō* in the pre-Christian period were found in Jewish religious writings. Moreover, Christianity began within the context of Judaism. It is, therefore, important to examine the types of music present in Jewish worship in order to determine the setting for the music practices of the New Testament church. The historical evidence about the Jewish performance of religious music coincides with the linguistic indication studied earlier.

Instrumental music accompanied the sacrifices in the Old Testament, and that by divine authority (Numbers 10:10; 2 Chronicles 29:20-36). David was responsible for organizing the ministry of music in the Old Testament (1 Chronicles 16:4; 23:5). Instrumental music was an important characteristic of the worship at the Temple, as the Book of Psalms indicates. This feature appears, if anything, to have become even more prominent in the second temple, after the return from exile. 1 Esdras 5:58-65 relates that on the rebuilding of the Temple under Zerubbabel and Jeshua "hymning the Lord" was accompanied by instruments. Temple worship at the beginning of the Christian era is described in both the Apocrypha and the Talmud.

Sirach in the second century B.C. in his description of the activities of the high priest Simon has left a summary of the procedures on the Day of Atonement:

> When he put on his glorious robe and clothed himself with superb perfection and went up to the holy altar, he made the court of the sanctuary

glorious. And when he received the portions from the
hands of the priests, as he stood by the hearth of the
altar with a garland of brethren around him, he was
like a young cedar on Lebanon; and they surrounded
him like the trunks of palm trees, all the sons of
Aaron in their splendor with the Lord's offering in
their hands, before the whole congregation of Israel.
Finishing the service at the altars, and arranging the
offering to the Most High, the Almighty, he reached
out his hand to the cup and poured a libation of the
blood of the grape; he poured it out at the foot of the
altar, a pleasing odor to the Most High, the King of
all. Then the sons of Aaron shouted, they sounded
the trumpets of hammered work, they made a great
noise to be heard for remembrance before the Most
High. Then all the people together made haste and
fell to the ground upon their faces to worship their
Lord, the Almighty, God Most High. And the singers
praised him with their voices in sweet and full-toned
melody. And the people besought the Lord Most
High in prayer before him who is merciful, till the
order of worship of the Lord was ended; so they
completed his service. Then Simon came down, and
lifted up his hands over the whole congregation of the
sons of Israel, to pronounce the blessing of the Lord
with his lips and to glory in his name. (50:11-20)[25]

The Mishna, compiled in the second century A.D.,
contains a detailed account of the regulations for the daily
burnt offering in its tractate Tamid. Tasks of the priests for
the day were assigned by lot. No sacred vessel was touched
before one washed his hands and feet in the laver. The ashes
and remains from the preceding day's sacrifices were removed
from the altar, the lamb was prepared and slaughtered by an
elaborate ritual. Offerings of fine flour, griddle-cakes, and
wine accompanied the burnt offering. A blessing was pronounced, the ten commandments recited, the *shema* (a
confession of faith in the one God) was spoken, and other
benedictions pronounced. Then the altar of incense was
prepared and incense was burned. The ceremony closed with
the high priest or other priests pronouncing the priestly
benediction of Numbers 6:24-26. Instructions are given for
the times when trumpets were blown, cymbals struck, and a
psalm chanted by the Levites. The tractate closes with a list

---

[25]The translation is that of the Revised Standard Version.

of psalms which were chanted in the temple on which days. The tractate Sukkah 5 in reference to the rejoicing at the Feast of Tabernacles states as follows:

> And Levites without number with harps, lyres, cymbals, and trumpets and other musical instruments were there upon the fifteen steps leading down from the court of the Israelites to the court of the women, corresponding to the fifteen songs of ascents in the Psalms [120-134]. It was upon these [and not at the side of the altar where they performed at the time of the offering of sacrifices] that the Levites stood with their instruments of music and sang their songs.[26]

Instrumental music, therefore, was an important feature of the temple worship, and it was closely associated with its sacrificial system. Here may be a significant clue explaining the absence of instrumental music in early Christian worship. Early Christianity saw the sacrificial system and temple worship as superseded by the sacrifice of Christ and the worship of the church.[27] When the Levitical priesthood and the sacrificial cultus were abolished, naturally its accompaniments were too. Justin Martyr's *Dialogue with Trypho* 116-118 in the mid-second century speaks of Christians' "spiritual praises" replacing the Old Testament sacrifices (cf. the passage from Justin cited on p. 49). Accordingly, the incense which accompanied the offering of animal sacrifices became a symbol of the prayers of the saints (Rev. 5:8), but there is no reference to literal incense used in early Christian worship and several references in early Christian literature explicitly disown it.[28] Similarly something external and mechanical like instrumental music was superseded by the songs of praise. Any effort to justify instrumental music in Christian worship on the basis of its authorization in the Old Testament must reckon with its

---

[26] I have used the English translation by Herbert Danby, *The Mishna* (London: Oxford University Press, 1933).

[27] Bertil Gaertner, *The Temple and the Community in Qumran and the New Testament* (Cambridge, 1965), especially pp. 84ff.; R. J. McKelvey, *The New Temple: The Church in the New Testament* (Oxford U. Press, 1969), pp. 180, 183ff. for conclusions.

[28] Justin, *Apology* I, 13; Athenagoras, *Plea* 13; Irenaeus, *Against Heresies* IV.xvii.6; Clement of Alexandria, *Instructor* II.viii.67; Tertullian, *Apology* 30.

setting and function in the Temple cultus and determine whether that authorization can be detached from the Levitical order and sacrificial cultus.

At any rate the associations of instrumental music with the Temple were not favorable to its adoption by the early church. What then about the recitation of the Psalms, for they too were employed in the Temple? Here another factor entered the picture.

Synagogue Worship

In addition to the negative factor of instrumental music's association with the temple worship, there was the even more significant positive consideration of worship in the synagogue. The Jews had developed an alternative form of worship independent of the temple and animal sacrifice. It was the rational worship of prayer and Scripture instruction practiced in the synagogue. The synagogue had arisen as an independent institution in pre-Christian times. Its organization and procedures were well developed by the first century. Before the destruction of the temple the synagogue functioned as a complementary institution; after its destruction the synagogue continued as the permanent focus of Jewish religious life. Rabbinic literature preserves a report how on a festival day in the first century one's whole time was occupied:

> The first hour was occupied with the daily morning sacrifice; from there we proceeded to prayers; from there we proceeded to the additional sacrifice, then the prayers to the additional sacrifice, then to the House of Study [Synagogue], then the eating and drinking, then the afternoon prayer, then the daily evening sacrifice, and after that the Rejoicing at the place of the Water-Drawing all night.[29]

Rabbinic literature gives us only incidental references to early synagogue services, but the components and order can be reconstructed with a considerable degree of certainty,

---

[29]bSukkah 53a. Talmudic passages are cited from the translation edited by I. Epstein, *The Babylonian Talmud* (London: Soncino Press).

especially with the aid of the New Testament and Jewish writers such as Philo.[30] The principal features were prayer and the study of the Bible. The Scriptures were read with a melody or tune, called cantillation (bMegillah 32a).

Recitation or chanting of the Psalms is not so frequently mentioned, but seems certain for synagogue practice in New Testament times. Even as the priests and Levites were divided into twenty-four courses which took weekly turns in their service at the temple (1 Chron. 23-27; cf. Lk. 1:5, 8, 9), so Israel was divided. And when one's course of priests and Levites were on duty in Jerusalem, the corresponding laymen in Israel in their cities observed certain fasts and met daily for Scripture reading. Part of these daily services, according to the Mishna (Taanith IV), was the reciting of the Hallel Psalms (cf. Rosh Hashanah IV.7). The Talmudic commentary (bTaanith 27b-28a) refers to prayer and mentions that "they assemble in Synagogue."

Fortunately we are not dependent wholly on such incidental evidence. Jewish practice in the musical praise of God in New Testament times apart from the temple worship is preserved in both a contemporary account from Philo and in Rabbinic tradition in the Talmud.

Rabbinic comments of Exodus 15 describe three different types of responsorial rendition of vocal selections.

> Our Rabbis taught: On that day R. Akiba [early second century] expounded: At the time the Israelites ascended from the Red Sea, they desired to utter a song; and how did they render the song? Like an adult who reads the *Hallel* (for a congregation) and they respond after him with the leading word.[31] (According to this explanation) Moses said, "I will sing unto the Lord" and they responded, "I will sing

---

[30] Emil Schuerer, *A History of the Jewish People in the Time of Jesus Christ* (Edinburgh: T. and T. Clark, 1896), Vol. II, pp. 75ff.; I. Elbogen, *Der Juedische Gottesdienst in seiner geschichtlichen Entwicklung* (reprint Hildesheim: Georg Olms, 1962); Eric Werner, *The Sacred Bridge* (New York: Columbia U. Press, 1959), Part I; see also A. Z. Idelsohn, *Jewish Music in its Historical Development* (New York, 1944).

[31] Cf. bSukkah 38a for Hallelujah as a congregational response.

unto the Lord"; Moses said, "For He hath triumphed gloriously" and they responded, "I will sing unto the Lord." R. Eliezer [mid-second century], son of R. Jose the Galilean, declares, Like a minor who reads the *Hallel* (for a congregation), and they repeat after him all that he says. (According to this explanation) Moses said, "I will sing unto the Lord" and they responded, "I will sing unto the Lord"; Moses said, "For He hath triumphed gloriously" and they responded, "For He hath triumphed gloriously." R. Nehemiah [second century] declares: Like a school-teacher who recites the *Shema* in the Synagogue, viz., he begins first and they respond after him. On what do they differ?—R. Akiba holds that the word "saying" refers to the first clause; R. Eliezer, son of R. Jose the Galilean holds that "saying" refers to every clause; and R. Nehemiah holds that "and spake" indicates that they sang all together "and saying" that Moses began first. (bSotah 30b)

Prayers as well as the Psalms were performed responsively (bTaanith 16b).

Rabbinic literature preserves several accounts of controversy among Jewish teachers whether the essential part of temple music was instrumental or vocal. R. Simeon b. Eleazar [late second century] said, "The absence of Priests, Levites and musical instruments is a bar to the offering of the sacrifices." R. Jose said the essential feature of the music was the instrument, but Rab Judah held that the principal music at the temple was vocal (bTaanith 27a). In another place it is contended that slaves could play the instruments, but only Levites could sing because "the essential in the music of the Sanctuary was the singing with the mouth, the instrumental music being just for sweetening the sound." Others held that Levites were the players because instrumental music was essential. Rabbi Meir [second century] held that omission of the song invalidated the sacrifice, but the majority opinion was that it did not invalidate the sacrifice (bArakin 11a; cf. also bAbodah Zarah 47a).

The same discussion recurs in bSukkah 50b-51a with the added question whether playing on an instrument overrode the Sabbath prohibition of work.

"R. Jose is of the opinion that the essential feature of the (temple) music is the instrument, in consequence of which it is a Temple service which overrides the Sabbath, whereas the Rabbis are of the opinion that the essential feature of the (temple) music is the vocal singing, in consequence of which the (playing of the instruments) is not a Temple service and does not, therefore, override the Sabbath.

Elsewhere in Rabbinic literature instrumental music is forbidden on the Sabbath. In fact "one may not ring a bell or a clapper for a child on the Sabbath."[32] One factor here was that tuning an instrument would violate the prohibition of work. For instance, it was ruled that one might tie the string of an instrument in the Temple but not outside the Temple on the Sabbath (Erubin X:13; bErubin 104a). Hence it would seem that one consideration in the discussion of what was essential in temple music was to justify the place of instruments in the temple worship. Only if they were integral to the sacrifice could their use override the Sabbath law. In the absence of sacrifice there was nothing to permit the instrument to override the Sabbath law. Therefore, synagogue music was vocal. I venture to suggest that the discussion over instrumental music among the Rabbis was to justify its overriding the Sabbath in temple practice; but since their own music in the synagogue was vocal, they wanted vocal music to have been central and so insisted that the essential music of the temple also had been vocal. Accordingly, bSukkah 51a states, "All agree that the essential feature of the (Temple) music was the vocal singing." And the later *Midrash Rabbah, Numbers* VI:10 discusses only song as "an indispensible adjunct of sacrifice," even when citing passages which refer to instruments.[33] It was inferred from the phrase "in the name of the Lord" that ministering to God (Deut. 18:7) required song, because in song the name of the Lord was mentioned with praise and thanksgiving.[34]

The Rabbis gave definite expression to the view that vocal music was superior to instrumental. "The Holy One,

---

[32]Tosephata Shabbat XIII, cited in Alfred Sendrey, *Bibliography of Jewish Music* (Columbia Univ. Press, 1951), p. 348.

[33]*Midrash Rabbah, Numbers*, ed. H. Freedman and M Simon (London: Soncino Press, 1939), p. 175.

[34]This passage has some possible relevance for the Colossians and Ephesians descriptions of singing.

blessed be He, will say to them: Even though you praise Me
with psalteries and with harps, your praise is not sweet to Me
until it comes from your mouths" (*Midrash Tehillim On
Psalms* 149, 5). And again, "The Holy One, blessed be He,
said, I desire from Israel not music of the harp but the
solemn utterance of their mouth" (*on Psalms* 92, 7).[35] The
latter passage also allegorizes the ten strings as the ten men
required at religious services.

There were some efforts by the Rabbis to eliminate
instrumental music from other phases of Jewish life. Abstention from instruments was to be observed in mourning over
the destruction of Jerusalem. Some even wanted to outlaw
singing, but the Talmud concludes that "only musical
instruments are forbidden" at festivities (bGittin 7a; cf.
bSotah 48a). This abolition from entertainments, of course,
was not uniformly maintained.

These are later developments and discussions. They do
coincide with the absence of any evidence for instrumental
music in the early synagogue. The *shofar* (ram's horn) was
blown at fasts and New Year's, but it hardly counts as a
musical instrument and was not employed in the worship.
There remains no evidence that instrumental music was used
in the synagogue service; indeed this holds true until
comparatively recent times. The real reason for this absence
is probably that advanced by McKinnon,[36] namely that the
instrument was simply irrelevant to the type of worship
developed in the synagogue. It was a non-sacrificial worship
and a rational service to which, as an extension either of
prayer or of reading the Scriptures, had been added the
chanting of the Psalms.

Since a special vocal use of *psallō* is first and most clearly
attested in Jewish religious literature, and since the Psalms
were recited without instrumental accompaniment in the

---

[35] *The Midrash on Psalms*, trans. Wm. G. Braude (New Haven: Yale U. Press),
Vol. 2, pp. 383 and 114.

[36] James William McKinnon, *The Church Fathers and Musical Instruments*, an
unpublished doctoral dissertation at Columbia University, 1965, pp. 105-110.
Some of his evidence and conclusions is summarized in his article "The Meaning
of the Patristic Polemic against Musical Instruments," *Current Musicology*, Spring,
1965, pp. 69-82.

synagogue services, a reasonable hypothesis may be suggested for the change in the usage of the word. The change in practice in the synagogue, so that the Psalms were used without the instrumental accompaniment that had characterized their use in the temple, produced a change of meaning in the word so that it meant "to sing the Psalms." The difference in the way the Psalms were used changed the meaning of *psallō* which was employed to describe this use. Christians derived their use of the word from the Jewish circles in which the church began, not from classical Greek usage. Moreover, Christian worship in many of its practices seems to have followed the worship of the synagogue.

Philo on Music

The first century Jewish author Philo of Alexandria has left a full account of certain practices of the Therapeutae, a group of Jewish ascetics in Egypt akin to the Palestinian Essenes who produced the Dead Sea Scrolls. Not only does Philo's account of the worship of the Therapeutae give a confirmation of synagogue practice earlier than what is found in the Rabbinic literature, but it is also a very circumstantial account (from an eyewitness?) of sectarian Jewish practice in the Hellenistic world.

In reference to one of the sacred banquets of the Therapeutae Philo gives this description:

> Then the President rises and sings a hymn [*aidei humnon*] composed as an address to God, either a new one of his own composition or an old one by poets of an earlier day who have left behind them hymns in many measures and melodies, hexameters and iambics, lyrics suitable for processions or in libations and at the altars, or for the chorus whilst standing or dancing, with careful metrical arrangements to fit the various evolutions. After him all the others take their turn as they are arranged and in the proper order while all the rest listen in complete silence except when they have to chant the closing lines or refrains, for then they all lift up their voices [*exechousi*], men and women alike. (*The Contemplative Life* 80)[37]

---

[37]The translations of Philo are those of F. H. Colson (in some cases slightly modified) in the Loeb Classical Library. Some of the musical descriptions are obscure, but the general description is clear enough.

I take it that the hymns by poets of an earlier day are the Old Testament Psalms, which are described accommodatively (as are the other elements in the account) in accordance with Philo's custom in terms familiar to the Greeks. Eusebius of Caesarea, the fourth century church historian, summarizes the passage as follows:

> While one sings [*epipsallontos*, which by virtue of Philo's original can only mean "sing"] ..., the rest listen in silence and join in singing out the refrains of the hymns" (*Church History* II.xvii.22).

Philo's account of an all-night vigil by the Therapeutae gives further information on the manner of the singing. The fullness of the description rules out the presence of instrumental accompaniment.

> They form themselves into two choirs, one of men and one of women, the leader and precentor chosen for each being the most honored among them and also the most musical. Then they sing hymns [*aidousi humnous*] to God composed of many measures and set to many melodies, sometimes chanting together [*sunechountes*], sometimes taking up the harmony antiphonally, hands and feet keeping time in accompaniment, and rapt with enthusiasm reproduce sometimes the lyrics of the procession, sometimes of the halt and of the wheeling and counter-wheeling of a choric dance ... Then they mix and both together become a single choir, a copy of the choir set up of old beside the Red Sea in honor of the wonders there wrought .... This wonderful sight and experience ... so filled with ecstasy both men and women that forming a single choir they sang hymns of thanksgiving to God their Savior, the men led by the prophet Moses and the women by the prophetess Miriam. (*The Contemplative Life* 83-87).

This information from Philo has a double value. First, it shows how synagogue practice was adapted in the worship of sectarian Judaism, and it is the Jewish sects, such as the Essenes, which offer us generally the best parallels for understanding the early church. Second, Eusebius testifies that Philo's account of the precentor reciting the text and the congregation joining in a unison repetition of the closing words of a verse, so-called responsorial psalmody "exactly agrees with the manner which is still observed by us" Christians (*Church History* II.xvii.22).[38] Indeed Eusebius quotes extensively from Philo on the mistaken assumption that he was describing the early Christians.

Philo's extensive writings permit us to gain a full picture of the way Jewish religious and Greek philosophical thought on the subject of music flowed together at the beginning of the Christian era. Philo does not say much about instrumental music. Generally, instruments are allegorized or used as an illustration of harmony. *On Husbandry* 79-82 is one of Philo's frequent references to Exodus 15 and the duty to sing to God suitable hymns. Understanding the choruses of men and women in the text as respectively mind and sense perception, Philo continues,

> For it is right with both mind and sense to render hymns and sing blessings to the Godhead without delay, and tunefully to strike each of our instruments, that of mind and that of sense perception, in thanksgiving and honor paid to the only Savior.

Allegorical Laws I.v.14 calls the "seven stringed lyre the best of instruments" in a section praising the number seven (cf. *On the Creation* 126). *Life of Moses* I.29 says Moses' speech and life were in harmony and so "made melody together as on a musical instrument." Normally the comparison is to the harmony within the soul (*Posterity of Cain* 88; *Sacrifices of Abel and Cain* 74), or once a soul out of tune is like a lyre out of tune (*On Drunkenness* 116). The lyre is a symbol of harmony among diverse men in *Cherubim* 110.

Philo speaks negatively of the use of instruments to arouse lust in *Special Laws* II.193, and of all poetry and music in the service of idolatry in the same work, I.28f. Pleasure caused by instruments is inferior because irrational (*Allegorical Laws* II.75; III.221). There is a further disparagement of instruments in *On Flight and Finding* 22. Philo disparages instrumental in comparison to vocal music:

---

[38]For this method of singing see my *Early Christians Speak* (Austin: Sweet Publishing Co., 1971), pp. 161, 164.

> All the melodious sounds produced by wind-and
> stringed-instruments fall as far short of the music that
> comes from nightingales and swans, as a copy and
> imitation falls short of an original, or a perishable
> species of an imperishable genus. For we cannot
> compare the music produced by the human voice
> with that produced in any other way, since it has the
> pre-eminent gift of articulation, for which it is prized.
> (*Posterity of Cain* 105)

Such praise of vocal music is most characteristic. Happy
is the man who uses "the organ of his voice to laud both the
world and its Maker" (*Who Is the Heir?* 111). In *Noah's Work
as a Planter* 135 Judah is allegorically understood as "the
mind that blesses God and is ceaselessly engaged in singing
thanksgiving hymns to him" (cf. *On Dreams* II.34 where
Judah is also interpreted of "songs and hymns" to God). The
exaltation of Judah in the passage is concluded with the
declaration that "of all truly right actions the best and most
perfect is the hymn of praise to the Father of the universe."

On the other hand, Philo recognized that even the voice
is inadequate to the praise of God.

> O Lord and Master, how can one hymn thee?
> What mouth, what tongue, what else of the instru-
> ments of speech, what mind, soul's dominant part, is
> equal to the task? (*Life of Moses* II.239)

Hence, there occurs in a few passages the concept of "silent
singing" as the highest type of praise. The treatise *On
Drunkenness* 94 takes up the interpretation of Judah again,
this time as the leader of those who "raise the hymn of
thanksgiving with their hearts rather than with their voices."
Noah's Work as a Planter 126 depreciates buildings, gifts, and
sacrifices as expressions of gratitude to God: "it must be
expressed by means of hymns of praise, and these not such as
the audible voice shall sing, but strains raised and re-echoed
by the mind too pure for eye to discern." *Special Laws* I.272
has both vocal and silent praise in a passage giving fine
expression to one of Philo's noblest thoughts:

> And indeed though the worshippers bring noth-
> ing else, in bringing themselves they offer the best of
> sacrifices, the full and truly perfect oblation of noble
> living, as they honor with hymns and thanksgivings

their Benefactor and Savior, God, sometimes with the
organs of speech, sometimes without tongue or lips,
when within the soul alone their minds recite the tale
or utter the cry of praise. These one ear only can
apprehend, the ear of God.

"Silent singing" was advocated in certain philosophical circles
of the Hellenistic world but was never a strong option in
Judaism or Christianity.

The verb "to hymn" is often used by Philo to mean "to
praise" or "extol" with no musical connotation—*On the
Virtues* 22; 187; *The Worse Attacks the Better* 73; *On the
Change of Names* 196. Hence, he specifies "song" when that
is the type of praise intended, as "to hymn with a song" (*On
the Virtues* 72) and "Moses in the Song hymns God" with
reference to Exodus 15 (*Allegorical Laws* II.102).

Philo very often has "odes and hymns" together, and
frequently with a third term. Jacob assigned to Judah "praise
and hymns and hallowed songs [*odas*] from his brethren"
(*Allegorical Laws* III.26). *Life of Moses* II.162 on the
incident of the golden calf offers a parallel to Ephesians
5:18f.:

They offered sacrifices which were no sacrifices,
set up choirs which were no choirs, sang hymns which
were very funeral chants, and filled with strong drink,
were overcome by the twofold intoxication of wine
and folly." (Cf. "odes and hymns" in the account of
the same incident in *Special Laws* III.125.)

On Joseph 253 has the participle of *sunadō* with the verb
humneō. The combination songs (*asma*) and hymns occurs in
the account of the musical compositions of the Therapeutae
(*The Contemplative Life* 29). Philo's terminology offers a
confirmation of the observations made above (pp. 14, 15) on
the general interchangeability of words for vocal compositions.

Philo nowhere refers to instrumental music in reference
to Jewish religious music in his own day. But he does offer
descriptions of the singing, in addition to that of the
Therapeutae cited above. When the Jewish population of

Alexandria was delivered from a great peril, Philo recounts how they came together and "with hands outstretched to heaven they sang hymns and led songs of triumph to God." And further, "All night long they continued in hymns and odes" (*Flaccus* 121, 122). *On Drunkenness* 121 refers to the leaders of the song and the "precentors of the chorus which sings the hymn of thanksgiving." Antiphonal singing occurs twice in the *Life of Moses* (I.180; II.256f.). Philo refers to Exodus 15 and Moses dividing the nation into a choir of men led by himself and a choir of women led by Miriam to sing hymns of thanksgiving to God. That this is more than a historical reference by Philo is indicated by the frequency of his reference (which indicates the importance of the episode to him), the similar concern of the Rabbis with the passage (cited above), and by the exact parallel of his version of the Biblical story with his account of the practice by the Therapeutae in his own day which he holds up as a model.

The conclusion drawn from the New Testament texts and from linguistic evidence was that instrumental music was not present in the worship of the New Testament church. This conclusion has further support in the contextual setting of New Testament times. Jewish practices and attitudes (both Rabbinic and Hellenistic) furnish strong presumption against the presence of instrumental music in the early church. The next chapter will test this conclusion by the testimony of church history.

Before leaving the New Testament references, we may note in passing that the New Testament gives no negative judgment on instrumental music *per se*. It makes neutral references to playing on instruments (Matthew 11:17 and parallels), uses instruments as illustrations (1 Corinthians 13:1; 14:7f., with unfavorable connotations it may be noted), and compares the heavenly worship to the sound of instruments (Revelation 14:2f., probably under the influence of Old Testament and temple practice). A parallel to the last reference may be seen in Revelation 5:8 with its figurative use of incense from the temple worship. The situation is simply that instruments are not referred to in the church's worship.

QUESTIONS FOR STUDY

1. Describe the sacrificial worship of the Temple.

2. Does the association of instrumental music with animal sacrifice have any relevance for determining the practice of the New Testament church?

3. Does the use of instrumental music in Old Testament worship have any bearing on its use in the New Testament church? Suggest some other acts which were a part of Old Testament worship but not New Testament.

4. What do we know of the musical practices of the Synagogue? What was the attitude of the Rabbis toward instrumental music?

5. What was Philo's attitude toward music?

6. What significance does the practice of the Synagogue and of Jewish sects have for determining what was probably the practice of the early church? What was the religious and cultural setting of early Christianity—Judaism or Greek culture and religion?

7. Supplementing this book with a concordance or Bible dictionary, determine which musical instruments are referred to in the New Testament. In what circumstances are these references made?

CHURCH

HISTORY

Chapter II

THE TESTIMONY OF HISTORY

One means of testing an interpretation of New Testament texts is by the background sources. Both instrumental music and unaccompanied vocal music were present in the Jewish background of the early church. The immediate setting for early Christianity, the synagogue and sectarian Judaism, as we have seen, favored the practice of purely vocal music. Another means of testing the interpretation of the New Testament is by its foreground, the witness of early church history.

Have we read the New Testament correctly? This can be checked in part by the interpretation of the New Testament in early Christian writings and by the practice of the post-New Testament church. Is it an accident that we have no clear reference to instrumental music in the church's worship in the New Testament? Was instrumental music actually used but not referred to? The answer of history is "No." What is an inference from the New Testament evidence, and the presumption from the church's setting in the context of Judaism, is made explicit in the testimony from church history. When our conclusions about the New Testament evidence concerning the use of the instrument are checked by the writings of the early church, we once more find a negative result.

Singing in Christian Worship

We now assemble here some of the historical evidence concerning early Christian practice in worship.[39] We shall

---

[39]For other compilations of patristic evidence on church music, see the dissertation by MacKinnon in footnote 35; J. Quasten, *Musik und Gesang in den Kulten der Heidnischen Antike und Christlichen Fruehzeit* (Muenster, 1930); Théodore Gérold, *Les pères de l'églis et la musique* (Paris, 1931).

give the passages which refer to music in descriptions of corporate assemblies for worship. It is to be noted that there is a consistent reference to singing but an absence of any reference to playing.

Ignatius of Antioch (early second century) uses an instrument as an illustration of harmony[40] and then describes church unity in language influenced by actual worship practice, which included only singing:

> For your deservedly famous presbytery, worthy of God, is attuned to the bishop as strings to a kithara.[41] Therefore by your concord and harmonious love Jesus Christ is being sung. Now all of you together become a choir so that being harmoniously in concord and receiving the key note from God in unison you may sing with one voice through Jesus Christ to the Father. (*Ephesians* 4)

Ignatius says in *Romans* 12:2, "Becoming a chorus in love you may sing to the Father in Christ Jesus." We may lay alongside Ignatius' use of an instrument in a comparison the figurative use in the contemporary *Odes of Solomon* 6:1:

> As the hand moves over the harp, and the strings speak, so speaks in my members the Spirit of the Lord, and I speak by his love.[42]

Ignatius' stress on congregational singing as done with "one voice" is characteristic of early Christian literature.[43] This may be due to the predominantly monophonic nature of early Christian singing, but there are enough references to the different pitches of the voices of male and female, old and

---

[40]This was a common rhetorical figure of speech which we have already found in Philo. It was fairly frequent in early Christian authors, for example Irenaeus, *Against Heresies* II.xxv.2. Jerome compared many singing together in unison to the "cithara which with many separate chords produces one sound" (*Homily* 65, *On Psalm* 87 [88], English translation in Fathers of the Church, Vol. 57, p. 56).

[41]Ignatius, *Philadelphians* 1:2 speaks of "attuned to the commandments as strings to a harp."

[42]Translation from J. R. Harris and Alphonse Mingana, *The Odes of Solomon* (London, 1916). It is difficult to tell because of the poetic language whether the harp in 26:3 is literal or figurative.

[43]J. Quasten, *op. cit.*, pp. 91-102.

young, that this feature cannot be pressed in regard to the musical practice. The Christian authors always use the "one voice" idea (Rom. 15:6) in connection with unity and harmony in the church produced out of a diversity of sounds.[44]

The second-century sermon known as *2 Clement* exhorts, "Let us then give him praise not from the mouth only, but also from the heart" (9:10).

Justin Martyr in the middle of the second century refers to Jesus singing hymns in the midst of the apostles *(Dialogue with Trypho* 106). With regard to Christian practice he says:

> We praise [the Maker of the universe] as much as we are able by the word of prayer and thanksgiving for all the things with which we are supplied, since we have learned that the only honor worthy of him is not to consume with fire the things made by him for our sustenance but to use them for ourselves and those in need and, being thankful in word, to send up to him honors and hymns for our creation, all the means of health, the various qualities of the different classes of things, the changes of the seasons, while making petitions for our coming into existence again in incorruption by reason of faith in him. (*Apology* I, 13)

Justin may be using "hymns" in the sense of "praises," without any musical reference. The vocal content, however, is clear. There is a close parallel in the Christianized *Sibylline Oracles*, which shows what was included in the rejection of animal sacrifice. The following passage has been dated in the second century:

> Wherefore we, sprung of the holy race of Christ
> . . .
> Never are we allowed to approach the inner shrine of temples
> Or pour libations to images, or honor them with prayers,
> Or with the manifold fragrance of flowers or with the gleam
> Of torches, nor yet to furnish them with offerings of loaves;
> Nor to send up the flame of the altar with vapors of incense,
> Nor upon libations of bull-sacrifice to send the blood
> of slaughtered sheep,
> . . .
> But with holy understandings, rejoicing with merry heart,
> With abundant love and with generous hands,
> In gracious psalms and songs meet for God

---

[44] Cf. Clement of Alexandria, *Exhortation to the Heathen* IX.88.

To hymn thee the immortal and faithful are we bidden.
(VIII, 482-499)[45]

Justin's *Dialogue with Trypho* 116-118 makes the same contrast of "spiritual praises" with the Old Testament sacrifices.

At the end of the second century Clement of Alexandria makes specific reference to what was done in the Christian assembly and in the context shows his vocal use of *psallō* (which has been demonstrated above). Clement castigates the hypocritical practice of appearing pious in the assembly and becoming quite worldly on leaving the assembly:

> After having paid reverence to the discourse about God, they leave within what they have heard. And outside they foolishly amuse themselves with impious playing, and amatory quavering, occupied with flute-playing, and dancing, and intoxication, all kinds of trash. They who sing [*adō*] thus, and sing in response, are those who before hymned immortality,—found at last wicked and wickedly singing [*psallō*] this most pernicious palinode, "Let us eat and drink, for tomorrow we die." (*Instructor* III.xi.80,4)[46]

In the church one "hymns," and this is parallel to the *adō* and *psallō* done outside the assembly. One may note the company of the quite different act of flute-playing. In another passage Clement summarizes the acts of worship:

> Always giving thanks in all things to God through righteous hearing and divine reading, true inquiry, holy oblation, blessed prayer, praising, hymning, blessing, singing (*psallō*), such a soul is never separated from God at any time. (*Miscellanies* VI.xiv.113,3)

At the beginning of the third century Tertullian lists the acts of worship as "when the Scriptures are read, or the

---

[45]Translation from E. Hennecke, *New Testament Apocrypha*, Vol. II (London: Lutterworth, 1965), pp. 740f. The same document has a strong condemnation of instruments in VIII, 113, which will be cited later. Cf. with the present passage Athenagoras, *Plea for the Christians* 13.

[46]Translation from the *Ante-Nicene Fathers*, Vol. II, p. 290.

psalms are chanted, or sermons are preached, or prayers are sent up" (*On the Soul* 9:4). Tertullian also refers to the custom of an individual singing a hymn, either from the Scriptures or of his own composition, at the love feast *(Apology* 39:18). Hippolytus speaks of the "proper day . . . in the house of God" when "all are praying there and singing (*humneo*) to God" (*Commentary on Daniel,* PG 10:693D).

A fragment of a third century Christian hymn has been found among the Oxyrhynchus Papyri. It contains notations for vocal rendition but none for instrumental accompaniment.[47]

Eusebius summarizes Christian worship at the beginning of the fourth century by referring to the "singing of Psalms [*psalmodia*] and recitation of other such words as have been given us from God," "the ineffable symbols of the Savior's passion were present," and the church's rulers delivered orations, "inspiring the assembly" (*Church History* X.iii.3). He gives this information in his *Commentary on Psalms* 65:10-15:

> Throughout the world—in cities, in villages, and in the country—in all the churches of God the people of Christ, who have been chosen out of all the nations, send up, not to the native gods nor to demons but to the one God spoken of by the prophets, hymns and psalmody with a loud voice so that the sound of those singing [*psallontōn*] can be heard by those standing outside. (PG 23:657D-660A; cf. also 648A and 648D-649A)

Patristic authors fairly frequently stress that all participated and in unison when the Psalms were sung. Ambrose *On Psalm* 1, *Exposition* 9 states as follows:

> What a labor it is to achieve silence in church while the lessons are being read. When one man would speak, the congregation makes a disturbance. But when the psalm is recited it makes its own "silence," since all are speaking and there is no disturbance. Psalms are sung by emperors; the com-

---

[47]E. Wellesz, "The Earliest Example of Christian Hymnody," *Classical Quarterly* 39 (1945), pp. 34-45; Quasten, *op. cit.,* pp. 101f.; Gérold, *op. cit.,* p. 45. This and a selection of other early Christian hymns is translated in my *Early Christians Speak*, pp. 149-155.

mon people rejoice in them. Each man does his utmost in singing what will be a blessing to all . . . . Psalmody unites those who disagree, makes friends of those at odds, brings together those who are out of charity with one another. Who could retain a grievance against the man with whom he had joined in singing before God? The singing of praise is the very bond of unity, when the whole people join in song a single act of song. The strings of the harp are of varying lengths, but the harmony is a unity. The musician's finger, too, may often make mistakes on the small strings, but in the congregation that great Musician, the Spirit, cannot err.[48]

Ambrose defends women singing in the unquoted part, taking into account 1 Corinthians 14:34. Basil of Caesarea in Cappadocia, *Epistle* II.207,3, speaks of the singing of the Psalms in "all the churches."[1] He defends, in addition to the more customary responsorial singing, the practice of dividing the congregation into two parts for antiphonal singing. For the latter he uses the word *antipsallō*. "All in common," he says, "as from one mouth and one heart offer up the psalm of confession to the Lord" (PG 32:764A-B). Chrysostom gives an important testimony in his *Homily XXXVI On 1 Corinthians* 14:33:

> They all met together in old time and sang refrains [*upepsallon*, "responded to the Psalms"] in common. This we do also now, but then among all there was one soul and one heart. (PG 61:313)[49]

The Non-Use of An Instrument

The conclusion that the early church did not employ instrumental music in worship does not rest, however, on inferences from silence. There are explicit statements from early Christian writers to the effect that Christians did not use instrumental music. Lest anyone be misled by citations which might *imply* a use of instrumental music in the church,

---

[48]I have followed the translation of Erik Routley, *The Church and Music* (London: Duckworth, 1950), p. 229.

[49]Cf. the translation in *Nicene and Post-Nicene Fathers*, Series 1, Vol. 12, p. 220. Chrysostom *On Psalms* 41 (PG 55:156-157) also stresses that all sing and emphasizes the value of the Psalms as replacing demonic songs. He uses *psallō* in the passage.

I cite here some of the explicit evidence against such use. Although it would be bold to say that an instrument was never used by Christians in their public assemblies, I can say that if it was, it was exceptional and unusual.

Statements written near the year 400 from both the Greek and Latin halves of Christendom declare the absence of instrumental music in Christian worship. The anonymous *Questions and Answers for the Orthodox* is now ascribed to Theodoret, bishop of Cyrrhus in Syria.

> 107. Question: If songs were invented by unbelievers to seduce men, but were allowed to those under the law on account of their childish state, why do those who have received the perfect teaching of grace in their churches still use songs, just like the children under the law?
>
> Answer: It is not simple singing that belongs to the childish state, but singing with lifeless instruments, with dancing, and with clappers. Hence the use of such instruments and the others that belong to the childish state is excluded from the singing in the churches, and simple singing is left. For it awakens the soul to a fervent desire for that which is described in the songs, it quiets the passions that arise from the flesh, it removes the evil thoughts that are implanted in us by invisible foes, it waters the soul to make it fruitful in the good things of God, it makes the soldiers of piety strong to endure hardships, it becomes for the pious a medicine to cure all the pains of life. Paul calls this the "sword of the spirit," with which he arms the soldiers of piety against their unseen foes, for it is the word of God, and when it is pondered and sung and proclaimed it has the power to drive out demons (PG 6:1354).[50]

Niceta, bishop of Remesiana in what is now Yugoslavia, wrote one of the first treatises on church music, *On the Utility of Hymn Singing*. He opposed the interpretation of those few who advocated "silent singing" in the church (chapter 2) and explained David's harp as a symbol of the cross of Christ (chapter 4). Between the extremes of silent singing and accompanied music he set forth the value of the

---

[50]The translation is that of William Green, "Ancient Comment on Instrumental Music in the Psalms," *Restoration Quarterly* Vol. I, No. 1 (1957), pp. 5f.

church's practice. Concerning the abolition of instruments he wrote as follows:

> It is time to turn to the New Testament to confirm what is said in the Old, and, particularly, to point out that the office of psalmody is not to be considered abolished merely because many other observances of the Old Law have fallen into desuetude. Only the corporal institutions have been rejected, like circumcision, the sabbath, sacrifices, discrimination in foods. So, too, the trumpets, harps, cymbals and timbrels. For the sound of these we now have a better substitute in the music from the mouths of men. The daily ablutions, the new-moon observances, the careful inspection of leprosy are completely past and gone, along with whatever else was necessary only for a time—as it were, for children. Of course, what was spiritual in the Old Testament, for example, faith, piety, prayer, fasting, patience, chastity, psalm-singing—all this has been increased in the New Testament rather than diminished. (9)[51]

Niceta then proceeded to refer to the New Testament passages on singing. The company in which Niceta puts instrumental music is notable.

Most of the statements commenting on the non-use of instruments in the church occur in contrasts of Old Testament with Christian practice. In commenting on the passages in the Old Testament which refer to worshipping God with an instrument, Christian authors had to offer an explanation. The Psalms especially offered a problem, for they were used in Christian worship. One approach is that taken by John Chrysostom and other writers of the Antiochian school of interpretation. God allowed the Jews to use instrumental music, even as he allowed animal sacrifice, not because that was what he desired, but as a transitional practice in leading people from idolatry to true spiritual worship. Theodoret, *On the Healing of Greek Afflictions* 7:16 on the subject of sacrifices is typical:

> So it was not in any need of victims or craving odors that God commanded them to sacrifice, but

---

[51] Translation by Gerald Walsh in Fathers of the Church, Vol. 7 (New York, 1949), pp. 71f.

that he might heal the sufferings of those who were sick. So he also allowed the use of instrumental music, not that he was delighted by the harmony, but that he might little by little end the deception of idols. For if he had offered them perfect laws immediately after their deliverance from Egypt, they would have been rebellious and thrust away from the bridle, and would have hastened back to their former ruin. (PG 83:997B)[52]

Similarly he says the following, *On Psalms* 150, 4:

"Praise him with psaltery and harp . . . ." These instruments the Levites formerly used when praising God in the temple. It was not because God enjoyed their sound, but because he accepted the purpose of their worship. For to show that God does not find pleasure in songs nor in the notes of instruments we hear him saying to the Jews: "Take thou away from me the noise of thy songs, for I will not hear the melody of thy instruments." He allowed these things to be done for the reason that he wished to free them from the deception of idols. For since some of them were fond of play and laughter, and all these things were done in the temples of idols, he allowed these things in order to entice them. He used the lesser evil in order to forbid the greater, and used what was imperfect to teach what was perfect. (PG 80:1996)

Chrysostom *On Psalms*149,2 says the following:

Many people take the mention of these instruments allegorically and say that the timbrel required the putting to death of our flesh, and that the psaltery requires us to look up to heaven (for this instrument resounds from above, not from below like the lyre). But I would say this, that in olden times they were thus led by these instruments because of the dullness of their understanding and their recent deliverance from idols. Just as God allowed animal sacrifices, so also he let them have these instruments, condescending to help their weakness. (PG 55:494).

Isidore of Pelusium also put the instrument in the same category with sacrifice: "If God allowed bloody sacrifices on

[52]This and the following two quotations are from Green, *op. cit.*, pp. 4-6. Theodoret in the same context once more puts instruments with sacrifice as displeasing to God (1001 B). In the same vein are his comments *On Isaiah* I, 11 (PG 81:225C).

account of the childhood of men, why do you marvel if also the music of the kithara and psalterion was played?" (*Epistles* II.176 in PG 78:628C).

Allegorical Interpretations of the Psalms

Another approach is alluded to in the quotation from Chrysostom above. That was to interpret the Old Testament references to instrumental music allegorically. As so much else in the Old Testament, instruments were not to be understood as having a literal place in Christian worship. Nevertheless, they had an allegorical significance which was still applicable to Christians. This approach is especially to be seen in writers under the influence of the Alexandrian school of interpretation, but was not confined to them. Chrysostom himself did some allegorizing *On Psalms* 150:

> Therefore, just as the Jews are commanded to praise God with all musical instruments, so we are commanded to praise him with all our members—the eye, the tongue, ear, the hand. Paul makes this clear when he says, "Present your bodies a living sacrifice, holy, acceptable unto God, which is your spiritual service." The eye praises when it does not gaze licentiously, the tongue when it sings [*psallē*], the ear when it does not listen to wicked songs and accusations against a neighbor, the mind when it does not devise treachery, but abounds in love, the feet when they do not run to do evil, but to carry out good works, the hands when they are stretched out, not for robbery and grasping and blows, but to give alms and to protect those who are wronged. Then man becomes a tuneful lyre, offering up to God a harmonious and spiritual melody. Those instruments were then allowed because of the weakness of the people, to train them to love and harmony. (PG 55:497)[53]

Even where he tries to draw direct lessons from the Psalms for Christians, Chrysostom does not go all the way with allegory:

> David at that time was singing [*epsalle*] in the Psalms, and we today with David. He had a kithara of

---

[53] *Ibid.*, p. 5.

lifeless strings; the church has a kithara arranged of living strings. Our tongues are the strings of our kithara, putting forth a different sound yet a godly harmony. For indeed women and men, old and young, have different voices but they do not differ in the word of hymnody for the Spirit blends the voice of each and effects one melody in all . . . .

The soul is an excellent musician, an artist; the body is an instrument, holding the place of the kithara and aulos and lyre . . . . Since it is necessary to pray unceasingly, the instrument is always with the artist unceasingly. (*Exposition On Psalm* CXLV.2, 3 in PG 55:521, 522).

Origen, from Alexandria and active in the first half of the third century, was a thorough-going allegorist, and many of the later interpretations of the Old Testament derive from him. The distinction he made between the psalterion and the kithara was to be the basis of many Patristic allegories.

The psalterion is the pure mind moved by spiritual knowledge. The kithara is the practical soul moved by the commandments of Christ. (*Selections on the Psalms* in PG 12:1552D)

The reason for this distinction, as later quotations will show, was that the psalterion produced its sound from the top of the instrument whereas the kithara produced its sound from the bottom of the instrument. After Origen's time it was standard to understand the psalterion as the higher part of man's nature and the kithara as the natural life. Therefore, the one had reference to intellectual or spiritual contemplation and the other to the practical life which involved obedience to commandments. So Origen comments on Psalms 33:2:

The kithara is the active soul being moved by the commandments of God, the psalterion is the pure mind being moved by spiritual knowledge. The musical instruments of the Old Covenant understood spiritually are applicable to us. The kithara, speaking figuratively, is the body, the psalterion the spirit. These are in tune for the wise man who employs the members of the body and powers of the soul as strings. He who makes melody [*psallon*] with the mind makes melody [*psallei*] well, speaking spiritual songs and singing in his heart to God . . . . The

> ten-stringed psalterion is the body, having five senses
> and five powers of the soul. (PG 12:1304B-C)

Origen appears to draw on his Greek learning in his use of *psallō*, for he seems to reflect the instrumental background of the word, nonetheless understanding the word figuratively. I think that in the few places where Christian authors reflect the classical meaning of *psallō*, they give it a metaphorical meaning, as Origen does here and in his comments on Psalms 149:3:

> Those who put to death their members upon the earth and take the principalities and powers up to the cross to be crucified with Christ make melody [*psallousi*] on the timbrel to God. Those who are whole and harmonious do so on the psalterion, the spirit. (PG 12:1680C)

Psalms 150:3-5 offered broad scope for allegorizing:

> The trumpet is the contemplative mind or the mind which has believed the spiritual teaching . . . .
> The kithara is the active soul moved by the commandments of Christ. The timbrel is the putting to death of the passionate nature on account of the good. Chorus is the unison of rational souls speaking the same thing and not having a division. The strings are the agreement of the corresponding sounds of the virtues and the works. The organ is the church of God composed of contemplative and active souls. The pleasant sounding cymbal is the active soul captured by the desire for Christ. The cymbal of jubilation is the pure mind inspired by the salvation from Christ. (PG 12:1684B-D)

The timbrel was commonly to be associated with "putting to death" because it was made by stretching a skin over a ring. Several of these ideas, in one form or another, recur in later authors, but each has his own variations within the general pattern of interpretation.

Athanasius in the early fourth century repeats the interpretation of the ten-stringed psalterion as the five senses of the body and the five powers of the soul (*Exposition in Psalms* 32:1 and 143:9 in PG 27:164B and 544A). The instruments of the Old Testament are commonly related in some way to the human body, as in *Epistle to Marcellinus* 29

(PG 27:41A-B). Athanasius' treatment of Psalms 150 shows his likeness to and difference from Origen:

> "Praise him with the sound of the trumpet," by his preaching. "Praise him with psalterion and kithara." Hymning him by the grace of the Holy Spirit with heart, tongue, and your lips. "Praise him with timbrel and dance." Hymn him by putting to death your entire body. "Praise him with strings and organ." Strings, I think, are nerves. When these are dead, and attached to a certain piece of wood, and played by a musician, they make a sound. The organ is pipes which are brought together and share with one another the melody blown by the breath when someone plays on them. Praise him then in the light commandments and the hard—in those things which are lacking by the mortification of the body and in the love which is effected by the Holy Spirit .... "Praise him with pleasant cymbals." Hymn him with the lips of your body. (*On the Titles of the Psalms* 150 in PG 27:1341B-D)

In his *Exposition in Psalm* 97, 5 Athanasius explains that "He calls kithara the harmony of the body with the soul .... He signifies by the trumpets the fervent and prolonged preaching of the gospel" (PG 27:42OC). Later Hesychius of Jerusalem, *On the Psalms* 97, makes the kithara the Old Testament and the trumpet the Gospels (PG 93:1268A-B).

Basil of Caesarea later in the fourth century in his *Homily on Psalms* 32, 2 (English 33:2) picks up the etymological use of *psallo* from the text of the Psalm but treats it metaphorically as he develops the common allegories:

> It is necessary to praise the Lord first with the kithara, that is to perform harmoniously the deeds done through the body .... Then after this confession you are worthy to praise [*psallein*] God on the ten-stringed psaltery. For it is necessary first to perform right actions with the body so as to act harmoniously with the divine word, and in this way to ascend to the contemplation of spiritual things. For the mind which seeks the things above is called the psalterion, because in the construction of this instrument the power of sound comes from the upper parts .... He who observes all the commandments and makes a symphony of them is the one who praises [*psallei*] God on the ten-stringed psaltery, because

ten was the number of the commandments written at
the first giving of the law. "Sing to the Lord a new
song." That is, serve God not in the oldness of the
letter but in the newness of the spirit. He who
receives the law bodily but understands it spiritually
is the one who sings the new song. That which
becomes old of the covenant departs, but the new
and renewing song of the Lord's teaching has been
delivered to us. (PG 29:325C-328B)

Basil's *Homily on Psalm* 1, 2 (PG 29:213B-C) also notes that
the psalterion sounds from the higher part, but the lyre and
kithara are sounded by the plectron from below.

Basil's brother, Gregory of Nyssa, is generally more
original than most authors in his treatment of Scripture. *On
the Titles of the Psalms* I.ix shows this originality, but within
the generally accepted framework of interpretation:

He says, "Praise the Lord with the sound of the
trumpet," when he represents the perfect harmony in
the full variety of virtues, as human ability becomes
an instrument in the rhythm of its music to God. The
Word names this instrument, figuratively speaking, a
psalterion and kithara. This human ability puts aside
everything earthly, dumb, and speechless and adds
the sound of its own strings to the heavenly choruses.
The strings stretched on an instrument would be the
tautness which does not give way to evil in each
virtue. The beautiful sound of the cymbal blended
with the strings occurs when the sound of the
cymbals arouses the desire for the divine chorus.

The emphasis on virtue attained by human ability is
characteristic of Gregory's spiritual writings in the later
period of his life.

The historical and the allegorical interpretations are
united in an important statement from Eusebius. His *Commentary on Psalms* 91:2, 3 contains many of the emphases
characteristic of the patristic testimony on our subject:

Of old at the time those of the circumcision were
worshipping with symbols and types it was not
inappropriate to send up hymns to God with the
psalterion and kithara and to do this on Sabbath days
(breaking the rest and transgressing the law concern-

ing the Sabbath). But we in an inward manner keep the part of the Jew, according to the saying of the apostle .... (Romans 2:28f.) We render our hymn with a living psalterion and a living kithara, with spiritual songs. The unison voices of Christians would be more acceptable to God than any musical instrument. Accordingly in all the churches of God, united in soul and attitude, with one mind and in agreement of faith and piety, we send up a unison melody in the words of the Psalms. We are accustomed to employ such psalmodies and spiritual kitharas because the apostle teaches this saying, "in psalms and odes and spiritual hymns." Otherwise the kithara might be the whole body, through whose movements and deeds the soul renders a fitting hymn to God. The ten-stringed psalterion might be the worship performed by the Holy Spirit through the five senses of the body (equalling the five powers of the soul). (PG 23:1172D-1173A)

The Greek interpretations found their way into Latin authors. Jerome reflected the common allegories of words when he defined *cantare* in Scripture as

sing meditatively, that is, to think about the mystery and the sense of divine Scripture. 'Psallere,' on the other hand, implies the chanting of praise to God through a good work: for example, that the sense of hearing offer its service, and likewise the mouth, and the eyes, and the hands, all the members of the body harmonize, as it were, and thereby pluck the chords of the psaltery in noble acts. (*Homily* 7 *On Psalm* 67 [68])[54]

His *Homily* 21, *On Psalm* 91 [92] employs the idea of the person as the instrument:

'With ten-stringed instrument and lyre, with melody upon the harp,' I shall paraphrase this in simple language: Whenever we lift up pure hands in prayer, without deliberate distractions and contention, we are playing to the Lord with a ten-stringed instrument .... Our body and soul and spirit—our harp—are all in harmony, all their strings in tune.

---

[54] The translation of this and the following two selections from Jerome is by Marie Liguori Ewald, *The Homilies of Saint Jerome*, Vol. 1, in The Fathers of the Church, Vol. 48 (Washington, 1964), pp. 51, 166, and 358. For this passage one may compare Chrysostom, *Homily* IX *on Colossians* 3, 16 and elsewhere, where he presents hymnody as superior to psalmody. The idea is discussed below, pp. 72, 73.

Similarly his *Homily* 48, *On Psalm* 136 [137]:

> Just as the shepherd's pipe is composed of many
> reeds but sends forth one harmonious tune, even so,
> we have our own musical instrument on which to
> play, and by means of it, through works, we offer a
> tune, a song, a hymn to God. By analogy, too,
> through our sense of hearing, through smell, taste,
> sight, and through all our faculties, we offer a hymn
> and a song to the Lord as from a single instrument.

The idea that the true praise of God is in doing his will
appears frequently in Augustine, as in *Expositions on Psalms*
XXXIII,2:

> "Praise the Lord with harp:" praise the Lord,
> presenting unto Him your bodies a living sacrifice.
> "Sing unto Him with the psaltery of ten strings" (ver.
> 2): let your members be servants to the love of God,
> and of your neighbour, in which are kept both the
> three and the seven commandments.[55]

On Psalms XCII, 5 the psalterion of ten strings is the ten
commandments, and "song" is the word and "harp" is work:

> If thou speakest words alone, thou hast, as it
> were, the song only, and not the harp: if thou
> workest, and speakest not, thou hast the harp only.
> On this account both speak well and do well, if thou
> wouldest have the song together with the harp.

Augustine worked many variations on the higher and
lower theme. His *Expositions on the Psalms* XLIII, 5 takes
the information on the construction of the instruments and
makes a different application from that of the Greeks to the
two parts of our nature:

> What is the meaning of "praising on the harp,"
> and praising on the psaltery? For he does not always
> do so with the harp, nor always with the psaltery.
> These two instruments of the musicians have each a
> distinct meaning of their own, worthy of our consid-
> eration and notice. They are both borne in the hands,
> and played by the touch; and they stand for certain
> bodily works of ours. Both are good, if one knows

---

[55]The Augustine quotations are taken from the *Nicene and Post-Nicene Fathers*, Series 1, Volume 8.

how to play the psaltery [*psallere*], or to play the harp [*citharizare*]. But since the psaltery is that instrument which has the shell (i.e., that drum, that hollow piece of wood, by straining on which the chords resound) on the upper part of it, whereas the harp has that same concave sounding-board on the lower part, there is to be a distinction made between our works, when they are "upon the harp," when "on the psaltery:" both however are acceptable to God, and grateful to His ear. When we do anything according to God's commandments, obeying His commands and hearkening to Him, that we may fulfill His injunctions, when we are active and not passive, it is the psaltery that is playing. For so also do the Angels; for they have nothing to suffer. But when we suffer anything of tribulation, of trials, of offences on this earth (as we suffer from the inferior part of ourselves; i.e., from the fact that we are mortal, that we owe somewhat of tribulation to our original cause, and also from the fact of our suffering much from those who are not "above"); this is, "the harp." For there rises a sweet strain from that part of us which is "below:" we "suffer," and we strike the psaltery [*psallimus*] or shall I rather say we sing and we strike the harp.

Augustine's approval of playing the kithara and the psalterion is actually an approval of the two types of activities which he sees symbolized by these instruments. Reflecting his rhetorical education, he keeps the classical meaning of the Latin *psallere*. My impression is that the classical meaning is more common in Latin Christian authors than in Greek. Nevertheless, Augustine uses the word metaphorically, and at the end redefines it in terms of the church's usage as "sing." On Psalms LXVI, 3 he defines *psallere* in the Latin Bible in this way: "To play [*psallere*] is also to take up an instrument which is called a psaltery, and by the striking and action of the hands to accompany voices." He then proceeds to allegorize: one praises God by living well and doing good works.

Another variation of the higher and lower interpretation appears in *Expositions On Psalms* LVII, 14 where Augustine compares the psaltery and harp to two kinds of deeds wrought by the Lord—miracles from above, and sufferings from below: "The flesh working things divine, is the psaltery:

the flesh suffering things human is the harp." In another direction on Psalms LXXI, 28 we read, "There seemeth to be signified by the psaltery the Spirit, by the harp the flesh."

Statements Favorable to Instruments

Granting that we are denied the omniscence which would permit us to say instruments were never employed in the early church's worship, we can say that one is hard pressed to find a reference to it. Cognizance is now to be taken of some statements which have been appealed to as evidence that instruments were used in the early church.[56] There is no claim for completeness, but I include the passages which I have found cited in the secondary literature on the subject. The passages known to me fall into certain categories, and I expect the explanation given of the following passages will apply if others could be cited.

The one early passage which speaks unambiguously in favor of Christians playing a musical instrument comes from Clement of Alexandria and has been studied earlier (*Instructor* II.iv.43,3– see p. 22). Clement is an exception to the general ecclesiastical condemnation of all instrumental music (see below), but his exception applies only to the lyre and kithara, an exception in keeping with a general philosophical tendency to regard the lyre as a more acceptable instrument from the standpoint of man's rational nature. It should be further noted that Clement's statement concerns what is done at a banquet in the home, not at a church service nor even at an *agapē* (love feast). His descriptions of what was done in the assembly and his general attitude toward instrumental music were cited earlier (pp. 21, 50).

The reference to a "flute-girl playing the flute" (actually the *aulos* or pipe) in *Acts of Thomas* 5-9 is similarly at a secular dinner. Thomas sang an ode; whether to her accompaniment is not clear. The Greek version of the *Acts* uses *psallō* and *humneō* for his singing, which was a distinct act from the girl's playing even if she accompanied him.

---

[56] Quasten, *op. cit.*, pp. 105ff., takes up some passages falsely used to support the presence of instruments in Christian worship.

Some passages cited are due simply to misunderstandings. Tertullian, *On the Crown* 8 says,

> Nay, if Mercury also first strung the chord to give forth melody, I will not deny, when listening to David, that this invention has been in use with the saints, and has ministered to God.[57]

As the usage earlier in the chapter shows, Tertullian by "saints" means the holy ones who lived before Christ, and so in the reference to David here Tertullian has in mind worship in the Old Testament. But more importantly, the whole context has to do with items of everyday life for which a pagan origin is claimed and whether they can be used at all by Christians. Tertullian includes musical instruments in these things which are not wrong in themselves. He says nothing about present practice in the assembly of the church.

At best, the passages appealed to do not speak of what Christians did when assembled in the church. The closest approximation is the *Vision of Paul* 29.[58] Paul, conducted through heaven, sees David "standing alongside the altar," holding "in his hands a psaltery and a harp," and singing "Hallelujah." When others hear David, they reply "Hallelujah." (David's beginning of the singing and the people's reply "Hallelujah" reflect church practice in the responsive singing of the Psalms, and chapter 30 of this work stresses the importance of everyone who is able to do so to join in the singing of Hallelujah as a means of blessing the Lord.) The angel guiding Paul explained to him:

> Just as it is done in the heavens, so it is done below, because it is not permitted to offer to God a sacrifice without David, but it is necessary for David to sing psalms at the time of the offering of the body and blood of Christ.

Some reflections are in order on this text. David is one of the many Old Testament righteous whom Paul encountered on his heavenly tour. Since each is identified in a characteristic

---

[57]Translation from the *Ante-Nicene Fathers*, Vol. III, p. 97.

[58]I follow the translation in Hennecke, *op. cit.*, Vol. II, p. 778.

way, it is to be expected that David would be identified with his harp. The author is perhaps influenced by the imagery of harps in heaven employed by the book of Revelation (15:2). The parallel between the heavenly and earthly worship apparently is in the singing of the Psalms of David at the time of the eucharist, even as David sings before the heavenly altar.[59] How far the author would carry his parallel is not certain: he makes no reference to the instrument in describing the earthly service, only to the singing of the Psalms.

Martin J. Wynagaarden in the *International Bible Encyclopedia*, Volume IV, p. 2494A, has translated Basil, Epistle 207, 3, as saying he had "the Psalms rendered by skilled precentors after the manner of the triumphal Odes of Pindar, the congregation joining at the closing verse, with the accompaniment of lyres." We have discussed this passage above (p. 52) noting Basil's description of a purely vocal activity. There is nothing in the Greek text corresponding to the quotation, unless the author has been misled into introducing the idea of lyres by the Greek word *antipsallō*. The evidence for the meaning of *psallō* in Greek ecclesiastical authors has already been given; the whole passage is accurately translated in *Nicene and Post-Nicene Fathers*, Series 2, Volume VIII, p. 247.

Jacob of Sarug relates that Ephraim Syrus, fourth century, instructed choirs of virgins to sing and "was a father and spiritual kithara player in their midst."[60] Regardless of the context in which the singing was done, it is doubtful that Ephraim can be said to have accompanied the choir on a literal kithara. The qualification "spiritual" and the normal ecclesiastical use of the instrumental metaphor suggests that Jacob was referring to Ephraim's role as the director of the choir.

---

[59] Augustine, *Retractions* II, 11 (37) relates that a certain Hilary opposed the practice which was introduced at Carthage of singing hymns from the Book of Psalms either before the oblation of the Lord's supper or during its distribution, and Augustine wrote against him in defense of the custom. This controversy may provide the setting for the present passage and explain its insistence that David was singing Psalms at the heavenly altar and that the same practice was to be observed at the earthly altar.

[60] Quoted by Quasten, *op. cit.*, p. 117.

Synesius of Cyrene, who was more Greek than Christian, in the early fifth century composed hymns to Christ for accompaniment by the lyre:

> I was the first to find the measure established in new harmonies wherewith to smite the strings of the lyre in praise of Thee, Blessed One Immortal, illustrious Offspring of the Virgin. (*Hymn* 7:1ff.)

> In a somewhat Dorian cadence, I will lift up a clear song on my ivory-inlaid lyre, in Thy honour, Blessed Immortal, Offspring Illustrious of the Virgin .... And grant me to raise hymns with the choirs of the holy, in honour of Thy Father, and to Thy supreme power, O Blessed One, I will chant my hymns again, I will sing a song to Thee again, and again, perchance, I shall attune this unstained lyre to Thee. (*Hymn* 8:1ff., 50ff.; PG 66:1612-13)[61]

Were these hymns for private use? The contents of *Hymn* 8 certainly indicate private or family use with its petitions for his sister, friend, wife, and self. His Epistle 94 refers to singing about justice with the lyre in the home (PG 66:1464A).[62]

It is possible that certain Gnostics or some on the fringe of the Christian movement employed instrumental music. Hippolytus quotes a hymn in use among the Naassène Gnostics:

> I will hymn Attis, son of Rhea, not with the buzzing sounds of trumpets, or of Idaean pipers, which accord with the voices of the Curetes; but I will mingle my song with Apollo's music of harps. (*Refutation of All Heresies* V.iv)[63]

Even if the passage is to be taken literally, one may wonder what a hymn to Attis has to do with normal Christian worship. It may be significant that those who were most

---

[61] Translated by Augustine Fitzgerald, *The Essays and Hymns of Synesius of Cyrene*, Vol. II (Oxford University Press, 1930), pp. 389, 390.

[62] English translation as number 95 in Augustine Fitzgerald, *The Letters of Synesius of Cyrene* (Oxford University Press, 1926), p. 183.

[63] Translated from *Ante-Nicene Fathers*, Vol. V, pp. 56f.

syncretistic in uniting Greek elements with Christianity should offer the best evidence for accompanied singing.

The hymn of Christ in the second century *Acts of John* 95 uses *sumpsallō* ("sing praise with") and contains a reference to the *aulos*. The act of *psallō* 'is a distinct act from blowing on the pipe. The hymn has Christ dancing with his disciples. Such seems unthinkable in orthodox worship of the time, but dancing is as likely as the use of an instrument. Once more we are dealing with a syncretistic tendency in a document whose orthodoxy is suspect.

By far the largest number of passages which may be cited for a favorable attitude on the part of the church fathers to certain instruments come from passages where instruments are used as an illustration of harmony or where an allegorical interpretation is given. We have seen how Ignatius of Antioch used the strings of an instrument as an illustration of the church's unity (p. 48). Such is fairly frequent and says nothing more about the church's practice than any other illustration drawn from contemporary culture.

Interpretations of the Word "Psalm"

Many passages in interpreting the Psalms define the different Greek words involving the *psal* root according to their etymology and so make reference to playing on an instrument. Musicologists and historians have not infrequently mistaken such statements for descriptions of contemporary practice, although recognizing that such flies in the face of all the other evidence and in some instances would contradict the other testimony of the authors cited. According to the etymology of the words and the practice of the Old Testament, the patristic definitions are quite correct. What is often overlooked is that the distinctions between the words being defined become the basis for an allegorical interpretation; there is no literal application to Christians. Moreover, it is never stated that the instructions being allegorized had anything to do with Christian worship. We cite representative passages with some fulness so that the reader can see their real import.

Possibly the first in this line of tradition is Hippolytus (third century). The passages of interest are printed among the *dubia* (works of doubtful authenticity) in the editions of his writings, so they may not be as early as the third century, but since the statements are typical, they are worth considering.

> This book of Psalms before us has also been called by the prophet the "Psalter," because as they say, the psaltery alone among musical instruments gives back the sound from above when the brass is struck, and not from beneath, after the manner of others. In order, therefore, that those who understand it may be zealous to carry out the analogy of such an appellation, and may also look above, from which direction its melody comes—for this reason he has styled it the Psalter. For it is entirely the voice and utterance of the most Holy Spirit. (PG 10:713B)

> It is likely, also, that a similar account is to be given of the fact, that David alone of the prophets prophesied with an instrument, called by the Greeks the "psaltery," and by the Hebrews the "nabla," which is the only musical instrument that is quite straight, and has no curve. And the sound does not come from the lower parts, as is the case with the lute and certain other instruments, but from the upper. For in the lute and the lyre the brass when struck gives back the sound from beneath. But the psaltery has the source of its musical numbers above, in order that we, too, may practice seeking things above, and not suffer ourselves to be borne down by the pleasure of melody to the passions of the flesh. And I think that this truth, too, was signified deeply and clearly to us in a prophetic way in the construction of the instrument, viz., that those who have souls well-ordered and trained, have the way ready to things above. And again, an instrument having the source of its melodious sound in its upper parts, may be taken as like the body of Christ and His saints—the only instrument that maintains rectitude; "for He did no sin, neither was guile found in his mouth." This is indeed an instrument, harmonious, melodious, well-ordered, that took in no human discord, and did nothing out of measure, but maintained in all things, as it were, harmony towards the Father. (PG 10:716D-717A)

> As there are "psalms," and "songs," and "psalms of song," and "songs of psalmody" [in the titles of

the Psalms] , it remains that we discuss the difference between these. We think, then, that the "psalms" are those which are simply played to an instrument, without the accompaniment of the voice, and (which are composed) for the musical melody of the instrument; and that those are called "songs" which are rendered by the voice in concert with the music; and that they are called "psalms of song" when the voice takes the lead, while the appropriate sound is also made to accompany it, rendered harmoniously by the instruments; and "songs of psalmody," when the instrument takes the lead, while the voice has the second place, and accompanies the music of the strings. And thus much as to the letter of what is signified by these terms. But as to the mystical interpretation, it would be a "psalm" when, by smiting the instrument, viz., the body, with good deeds we succeed in good action, though not wholly proficient in speculation; and a "song" when, by revolving the mysteries of the truth, apart from the practical, and assenting fully to them, we have the noblest thoughts of God and His oracles, while knowledge enlightens us, and wisdom shines brightly in our souls; and a "song of psalmody," when, while good action takes the lead, according to the word, "If thou desire wisdom, keep the commandments, and the Lord shall give her unto thee," we understand wisdom at the same time, and are deemed worthy by God to know the truth of things, till now kept hid from us; and a "psalm of song," when, by revolving with the light of wisdom some of the more abstruse questions pertaining to morals, we first become prudent in action, and then also able to tell what, and when, and how action is to be taken. (PG 10:717B-C)[64]

Hippolytus' literal etymology applies to the meaning of terms in the Old Testament text, and he explains what he thinks was the practice in Old Testament times. He clearly distinguishes his literal interpretation from his present application. The latter is in line with the allegorical interpretations we have found elsewhere in the contrast between instruments producing their sound from the upper or lower part of their construction. He adds the new element of distinction between psalms and songs. Since the former involves activity ("playing"), it represents the active life of good deeds; since

---

[64] Translation from the *Ante-Nicene Fathers*, Vol. V, pp. 199-201.

the latter involves the voice and is related to the intellectual nature of man, it refers to the contemplative life of meditation.

Eusebius' introduction to his *Commentary on Psalms* makes the definitions clearer and adds historical information, showing he has the Old Testament practice in mind:

> The Psalm seems to have been named from the psalterion, a musical instrument differing in shape from the kithara. Hence, a song plucked on an instrument is called a "psalm." An "ode" is the melodious speaking of words without an instrument. A "psalm of an ode" is used when the song takes the lead and the melody is playing by the psalterion; an "ode of a psalm" is the reverse. According to the histories of the Kings and Chronicles David the king, after the death of Saul, brought the ark of the covenant of the Lord . . . to Jerusalem. He selected by lot out of the tribe of Levi four singers of psalms who were leaders of the songs to chant psalms [*psallein*] and to sing before the ark of the Lord and to offer joyful sounds for confession and praise with the instruments in tune—odes, and stringed instruments, and percussion instruments . . . . They stood before the ark of the covenant of the Lord and chanted psalms [*epsallon*] and sang to the Lord, one with a kinura, one with cymbals, one with a kithara, one with a psalterion. In their midst stood the blessed David, the chief of the leaders of song, playing the psalterion with masterful hands. Each was singing and chanting psalms [*epsallen*] in an orderly manner to God by the Holy Spirit. Whenever the Holy Spirit came upon one of the leaders of the psalm singing, the rest stood and kept silence and then responded in unison to the one singing [*psallonti*] "Alleluia." (PG 23:72D-73B)[65]

One is inclined to translate the first three occurrences of *psallō* in the passage "play," because there is certainly instrumental accompaniment in what is described and Eusebius has earlier shown he has etymological meanings in mind. On the contrary, Eusebuis' usage elsewhere (pp. 23, 24) is vocal and the last occurrence in this passage is clearly vocal. Unless Eusebius has the general meaning "make melody" in

---

[65] Cf. the summary in similar words at the end of the introduction to the commentary—PG 23:76B.

mind, the new idea in *psallō* in addition to "sing" is that of singing the psalms (as our translation supposes) or the vaguer "praise."

Basil of Caesarea, *Homily on Psalm* 29, 1 makes the allegorical application of the definitions:

> The structure of the body is figuratively a psalterion and an instrument attuned musically for our hymns to God. The deeds of the body which are performed for the glory of God are a psalm, whenever by harmonious reason we accomplish nothing unmelodious in our actions. An ode is whatever is present of a higher and divine contemplation. "Psalm" is a musical word whenever it is played on an instrument rhythmically according to the principles of harmony. An "ode" is a melodious sound rendered harmoniously apart from the accompaniment of an instrument. Here then, since it is entitled "Psalm of an ode," we consider the words to intimate that action follows on contemplation. (PG 29:305B-C)

Later in the passage (Psalm 29, 3) Basil makes the church's practice and his own use of words clear:

> "Sing [*psalate*] to the Lord, his saints." It is not the one who brings forth the words of the psalm [*psalmou*] with his mouth who sings [*psallei*] to the Lord, but those who send up the psalmody with a pure heart, are holy, and preserve righteousness before God. These are able to sing [*psallein*] to God, following the spiritual rhythms harmoniously. (PG 29:312C)

There appears to be a contradiction between the interpretation of the psalterion and the kithara noted earlier, which makes the psalterion represent the intellectual part of man and the kithara the active part, and the present interpretation of psalm (the sound produced by the psalterion) as the active part of man's nature and inferior to the ode or contemplation. Aside from the fact that one should not look for complete consistency where allegory is concerned, there is a unifying principle in the idea of man's higher and lower natures, his contemplative and active aspects. Where the emphasis is on sounding from the upper part of the psalterion, then it represents the contemplative side of man and is superior; where the emphasis is on the physical activity involved in plucking the psalterion, then its sound (the psalm) represents the active life and so is inferior. No doubt furthering the latter understanding was the common interpretation of the body as in instrument (p. 72). A further explanation is that in one case the contrast is between two kinds of instruments, in the other the contrast is between an instrument and the voice. Vocal praise represents the higher activity and instrumental sounds the inferior.

Gregory of Nyssa, *On the Titles of the Psalms* II.iii, avoided the apparent contradiction by taking the term psalm as representing mental activity and ode as representing outward deeds:

> There is a distinction between psalm, ode, praise, hymn, and prayer. A psalm is the melody of a musical instrument. An ode is the expression with words of a melody made by the mouth. A prayer is a supplication brought to God with reference to something of concern. A hymn is the honor rendered to God for the good things which are ours. Praise includes a panegyric for the divine accomplishments . . . . The interpretation which by these designations leads us to virtue is as follows. The psalterion is a musical instrument making its sound from the upper parts of its construction, and the music from this instrument is called "psalm." Therefore the word which exhorts to virtue has a significance from the very shape of its construction, for it informs us that the life which is not characterized by earthly sounds is a psalm. I say "sounds" meaning "thoughts." Rather it has the pure and audible sound produced from the upper and heavenly parts. When we read "ode" we understand through a figure the respectable life with reference to outward things . . . . Whenever the good is accomplished, when practical philosophy accompanies contemplative philosophy, there is the ode of a psalm or the psalm of an ode. Whenever one of these terms is placed by itself before the praises, either the good according to the mind alone is signified by the word psalm or the activity and respectability in outward things is the interpretation of the word "ode."

The passage continues in a similar vein.

Although the applications may vary, the same principles are evident in other passages where definitions of psalm and associated words are given.[66] If one wants to insist on the etymological meaning of psalm, he must, as these definitions demonstrate, take only instrumental sounds, but this is flatly contradicted by the regular Christian use of the term for the words.

Condemnations of Instrumental Music

Tatian's *Oration against the Greeks* 8 puts Apollo and his Kithara in very bad company. This is typical of the ancient church fathers, who go beyond the New Testament in pronouncing a negative judgment of musical instruments.[67] They give an explicit condemnation to instrumental music. Sometimes such outbursts are taken as a proof that instruments were being used, at least by some Christians, in public worship. The principle is that what somebody opposes, somebody is doing. In this case the inference goes too far. There is no polemic against instruments in church. That is not under consideration. The condemnations are of the use of instruments at social functions—banquets, the theater, and other entertainments of pagan society—and in idolatrous worship. In view of the violent response to the immoral uses of instruments in social life and their cultic use in pagan religion, it becomes incredible that the instrument was present in the worship of the church. That surely would have brought condemnation, or at least called for explanation. But there is not even a comment to this effect.

Pagan cult and immorality are associated in a passage from the Pseudo-Clementine literature:

> But in process of time, the worship of God and righteousness were corrupted by the unbelieving and the wicked, as we shall show more fully by and by. Moreover, perverse and erratic religions were introduced, to which the greater part of men gave themselves up, by occasion of holidays and solemnities, instituting drinkings and banquets, following pipes, and flutes, and harps, and diverse kinds of musical instruments, and indulging themselves in all

---

[66] Hilary of Poitiers, *Instruction on the Psalms* 19-21 (CSEL, Vol. 22, pp. 15-17); Jerome, *Commentary in Ephesians* III, v. 19 (PL 26:561C-562A); Didymus the Blind, *Expositions on Psalms* 4, 1 (PG 39:1164D-1165A).

[67] See Gérold, *op. cit.*, pp. 88-100. For instrumental music in pagan cultic and social life see Quasten, *op. cit.*, chapters I, II, and V.

kinds of drunkenness and luxury. Hence every kind
of error took its rise. (*Recognitions* IV.xiii)[68]

Instruments were cited among the features of pagan
games and theatrical productions which came under Christian
censure (Tertullian, *On The Shows* 10; Pseudo-Cyprian, *On
The Shows* 7). Instruments were especially associated with
banquets, and the drunkenness and sexual immorality which
often accompanied them. Tertullian declares, "The command
'to sing to the Lord with psalms and hymns,' comes suitably
from him who knew that those who 'drank wine with drums
and psalteries' [Isa. 5:11f.] were blamed by God" (*Against
Marcion* V.xviii).[69] Note the contrast made between
Ephesians 5:19 and instruments, and the association made by
Tertullian of wine with the instrument. To keep people from
wine Paul counselled psalms and hymns, but instruments and
wine-drinking went together. Basil of Caesarea likewise
associated instruments with drunkenness and pointed to the
origin of instruments with Jubal, a descendant of Cain.[70]
The association of instruments with licentiousness is well
seen in the following attack on Greek practices: "There are
excessive banquetings, and subtle flutes which provoke to
lustful movements, and useless and luxurious anointings, and
crowning with garlands" (Pseudo-Justin, *Discourse to the
Greeks* 4).[71] The aulos in particular came under attack.
Epiphanius of Salamis said, "The aulos itself is an imitation
of the serpent through which the evil one spoke to Eve and
deceived her. For from the pattern of the serpent the aulos
was constructed in imitation for the deception of men"
(*Against Heresies* XXV, 4 in PG 41:325C-328A).

Therefore, the church fathers advocated psalms to
replace secular music in the home. Chrysostom's *Exposition
in Psalms* XLI.2, 3 is typical: "Let prayer be added after
psalmody in order that along with the soul we may also
sanctify our house itself." Then Chrysostom rebukes those

---

[68]Translation from the *Ante-Nicene Fathers,* Vol. VIII, p. 137. For the
company kept by instrumental music, cf. *Homilies* III, xxv, 3-4.

[69]*Ibid.,* Vol. III, p. 468.

[70]*On Isaiah* V, 155, 158, 160f. (PG 30:372D-384C).

[71]Translation from *Ante-Nicene Fathers*, Vol. I, p. 272.

who appeal to David with his kithara as justification for making their house into a theater. "You should make your home into a church. Here there is psalm, prayer, dance of the prophets, and spiritual understanding by the ones singing." Then he discusses the value of the words said. If one enters the sacred chorus of God, there is no need of a musical instrument, he declares. Finally, he declares that psalm singing can be engaged in at any time, even silently if need be:

> It is possible in every place and at every time to sing [*psallein*] according to the understanding . . . . If you are a craftsman, you are able to sing [*psallein*] while seated at your place of work and while working . . . . 3. It is possible without voice to make melody [*psallein*] with the inner mind. For we do not make melody [*psallomen*] to men, but to God who is able to hear the heart. (PG 55:158-159)

Chrysostom in another passage contrasts the aulos, kithara, and pipes at one banquet and the hymns and psalm-singing at the Christian one (*Homily* I *On Colossians* 1, 5 in PG 62:306). Gregory of Nazianzus, *Oration* V, *Against Julian* II, speaks of things Christians have in contrast to pagan practices and says: "Let us take up hymns instead of timbrels, psalmody instead of lewd dances and songs, thankful acclamation instead of theatrical clapping . . ." (PG 35:709B).

Pagan religions used instruments to accompany their sacrifices and to arouse the emotions of their worshippers. The Christian version of the *Sibylline Oracles* brings pagan cult and immorality close together when it says that in Hades

> They pour no blood on altars in sacrificial libations;
> Drum does not sound, nor cymbal clash,
> Nor much-pierced flute with its frenzied note,
> No sound of pipe bearing likeness to crooked serpent,
> No trumpet, messenger of wars, with barbaric sound;
> No drunkards in lawless revels or in dances,
> No sound of lyre, no mischievous device. (VIII.111-119)[72]

---

[72] Quoted from Hennecke, *op. cit.,* Vol. II, p. 729.

Arnobius was one of the bitterest opponents among the early Christians of pagan practices:

> But let there be, as you wish, honor in wine and incense, let the anger and displeasure of the deities be appeased by the immolation and slaughter of victims: are the gods moved by garlands also, wreaths and flowers, by the jingling of brass also, and the shaking of cymbals, by timbrels also, and also by symphonious pipes? What effect has the clattering of castanets, that when the deities have heard them, they think that honor has been shown to them, and lay aside their fiery spirit of resentment in forgetfulness? Or, as little boys are frightened into giving over their silly wailings by hearing the sound of rattles, are the almighty deities also soothed in the same way by the whistling of pipes? and do they become mild, is their indignation softened, at the musical sound of cymbals? What is the meaning of those calls which you sing in the morning, joining your voices to the music of the pipe? Do the gods of heaven fall asleep, so that they should return to their posts? (*Against the Heathen* 32)[73]

In contrast to the cultic associations of instrumental music with animal sacrifice, Christians put forth their own worship as the true rational sacrifice. Although the Christian's spiritual sacrifice was more often expressed as prayer, song also was viewed as a Christian sacrifice in contrast to heathen worship (see the passages cited on page 49). Tertullian wrote of prayer as the "spiritual victim" which abolished earlier sacrifices and Christians as the true priests whose prayers were a sacrifice, accompanied to the altar with "psalms and hymns" (*On Prayer* 28). Chrysostom gives this testimony:

> Since God ... set in motion every instrument, his call goes out to every kind and age of life to make melody—old women, men, young men, boys, women, all those who dwell on the earth, laying the foundation already for the new covenant .... Let us then praise God continually, not ceasing from giving thanks for all things, both through words and deeds. For this is our sacrifice and offering; this is the excellent service appropriate to the angelic life. If we

---

[73] *Ante-Nicene Fathers*, Vol. VI, pp. 430f.

continue hymning him in this way, we shall make our
way through the present life without stumbling and
we shall enjoy the good things of the life to come.
(*Exposition on Psalm* CL in PG 55:498)

In keeping with this thought the fragments on the Psalms (I,
1) ascribed to Hippolytus can speak of David's hymns
replacing the sacrifices instituted by Moses (PG 10:712B).

In view of these associations of instrumental music and
its contrast with psalm singing, we can understand the
incompatibility which Ambrose saw between the psalms and
playing on a harp:

> And so it is justly said, 'Woe unto them that rise
> up early in the morning and follow strong drink,'
> when they ought to be rendering praises to God; for
> this they should rise before the dawn and run to meet
> the Sun of righteousness, who visits his own and
> arises upon us if we have bestirred ourselves for the
> sake of Christ and not of wine and luxury. They are
> singing hymns—will you cling to your harp? They are
> singing psalms; what business have you with a
> psaltery and a drum? Woe indeed to you for
> abandoning your salvation and choosing death.[74] (PL
> 14:717)

The *Canons of Basil* provide that a precentor in the church
who learns to play the kithara and persists in playing it is to
be excluded from the church.[75] This negative judgment on
instrumental music goes beyond anything in the New
Testament. It surely is to be accounted for by the circumstances of the time. Is the setting of the times a sufficient
cause for the absence of the instrument from the worship of
the church?

The Significance of Culture

Philostratus, *Life of Apollonius* V. 21 well expresses the
pagan conception of the uses of instrumental music, speaking
of the *aulos*: "The mourner may have his sorrow lulled to
sleep, the one rejoicing may be made more cheerful, the lover
may become more passionate, and the sacrificer may become
more inspired and full of sacred song."

---

[74] Quoted from the translation by Routley, *op. cit.*, p. 230.

[75] Wilhelm Riedel, *Die Kirchenrechtsquellen des Patriarchats Alexandrien*
(Leipzig, 1900), p. 267.

The opposition of the church fathers to instrumental music may very well be put down to the circumstances of the time and especially to the immoral uses of this type of music. Is it possible to explain the absence of the instrument from the church's worship on similar grounds? If early Christian writers speak so harshly of instruments in social contexts, one can only imagine the outcry which would have been raised to their presence in a worship service. The fathers never conceived that possibility. But was this purely a cultural phenomenon?

The church's non-use of instrumental music is in strong contrast to the surrounding religious world. Any non-use of instrumental music was not in the same category with non-use of a public address system. Instrumental music was available and was part of the surrounding religious practices. Not only in paganism, but also in Judaism, instrumental music accompanied sacrifice and had a prominent part in the celebrations. Was it this very frequency with which instruments occurred in the surrounding religious world that led the early church to reject them? Did it want to distinguish itself from all around it?

This does not seem likely. Much of the evidence cited already points to another reason, which will be developed in the next chapter. Moreover, why was not song rejected too? The instruments accompanied song, and hymns were present in the sacrificial worship of paganism and Judaism. If the church were going to reject instrumental music simply because of its associations in the surrounding religious world, song should have been rejected too.

Surely more was involved in the absence of instruments from the worship of the church than merely a negative reaction to pagan religious practice. Where we can check the early church's attitude, it does not seem to have shown such sensitivity to the culture about it. It made its decisions on religious and moral grounds. There was no consistent pattern of reaction against or accommodation to the cultural life of paganism where the church's own life, worship, and practices were concerned. This can be demonstrated in regard to parallel practices.

A test has been made of the church's cultural sensitivity on a related matter—women singers in the worship.[76] The results are pertinent here. Women singers played an important role in the pagan worship, and singing by women had immoral connotations. If the church's attitude toward the instrument was determined by culture, it would be reasonable that the attitude toward women singers would similarly be influenced. If the church rejected instrumental music because of its use in pagan cultus and its immoral associations, it should have similarly rejected the liturgical singing of women. The parallel is enhanced by the fact that women did not sing in the synagogue service. A number of early texts speak of the congregational singing of all Christians present, including women.[77] But women had a prominent place in various heretical groups, and women choirs were organized. Thus many church writers came to voice opposition to any singing by women in church.[78] The church appears to have gone its own way in relation to the pagan cultus. The church had too strong a sense of superiority to react merely out of rivalry to its pagan environment. But the church, then as now, was very sensitive to new movements and departures in its own midst. What was done by heretics and schismatics exercised considerable influence on what the church did. The result was a strong tendency in the late third and fourth centuries A.D. to impose complete silence on women in church. One may contrast the situation as regards instrumental music, where there are no testimonies to its use nor efforts to stamp it out of the church.

The church, like Judaism, had its own form of music (psalm singing) and was conscious of the superiority of this medium. This positive factor counted for more than any negative reaction to the cultural context.[79]

---

[76] Quasten, op. cit., pp. 111f. The information is also available in his "The Liturgical Singing of Women in Christian Antiquity," Catholic Historical Review 27 (July, 1941), pp. 149-165.

[77] See the references on pp. 51, 52 to which may be added Ignatius, Ephesians 4; Eusebius, Commentary on Psalms 65, 1-2 (PG 23;647ff.); Chrysostom, Exposition On Psalms XLI (PG 55:156f.); Exposition on Psalms CXLV, 2 (PG 55:521), Exposition on Psalms CL (PG 55:498).

[78] Cyril of Jerusalem, Procatechesis 14, quoted on p. 25; Isidore of Pelusium, Epistles I. 90; cf. Jerome, Against Pelagians I. 25.

[79] This is the thesis of J. W. McKinnon, op. cit., note 35 above.

Later History

Historical evidence makes it most unlikely that an instrument can be found in *psallō* in the New Testament and shows that the absence of any clear reference to instrumental music in the church's worship in early days was not accidental. It was not mentioned because it was not there. There is no time when one can point to an original use of instruments in the church being abandoned.

It is quite late before there is evidence of instrumental music, first the organ, employed in the public worship of the church. Recent studies put the introduction of instrumental music even later than the dates found in reference books.[80] It was perhaps as late as the tenth century when the organ was played as part of the service. This makes instrumental music one of the late innovations of the medieval Catholic church. When introduced in the Middle Ages, the organ was still not part of the liturgy proper. That is, it did not initially accompany the hymn service, but was a separate item in the service. The type of chant employed left no place for instrumental accompaniment until new styles of music developed.

The introduction of the organ into the service came only in the Western branch of Christendom, not in the Eastern Orthodox branch.[81] The latter churches still do not use an instrument in worship. The few congregations among them under western influence which have accepted instruments have provoked reaffirmations of the Orthodox musical tradition. One of these, *Byzantine Sacred Music*, by Constantine Cavarnos,[82] is a fine collection of the Greek patristic evidence on church music. Cavarnos is more certain of how singing was actually performed in the early church than seems to be warranted by the evidence. He argues for

---

[80] See McKinnon, p. 269.

[81] Egon Wellesz, *A History of Byzantine Music and Hymnography* (Oxford: Clarendon Press, 1961).

[82] Published by the Institute for Byzantine and Modern Greek Studies, Belmont, Massachusetts, 1956.

monophonic singing as strongly as he argues against instrumental music. This type of singing, however, has no explicit mention in the New Testament. Even though this was probably the early mode of singing, to insist on it alone would be to bind one cultural form of musical expression on other societies and so deny the universality of the Gospel. Not to use modern part-singing, which was not available, is not the same thing as not to use instrumental music, which was available. In putting an inference from musical history on the same level with an inference from the New Testament, Cavarnos has weakened his case. The form of vocal expression certainly would be a cultural matter, and to make exclusive claims for Byzantine music would be a case of cultural captivity. Still, the Eastern Churches are an important witness to the fact of the purely vocal style of early Christian worship.

Even in the West the acceptance of instrumental music has not been uniform. I recall very vividly a visit to St. Peter's cathedral in Rome several years ago. A group of nuns entered the church singing, and the guide for our tour group explained that the great organ in the cathedral was played only at Christmas and not at regular services. The Roman church has preserved a tradition of vocal singing, although not as an exclusive practice.

When the Reformation came, the Lutheran and Anglican churches continued instrumental music from their Catholic past. The Reformed and Anabaptist branches of Protestantism eliminated the instrument as a Catholic corruption and only came to reaccept it (and then not uniformly) about the 18th and 19th centuries. Zwingli eliminated singing along with the organ in his reformation of Zurich. Some of the early Anabaptists at Zurich followed his lead and interpreted the New Testament texts as permitting only a "singing in the heart."[83] The major influence on Reformed churches came to be that of John Calvin, and the singing of the Psalms without instrumental accompaniment was the prevailing

---

[83] See the letter of Conrad Grebel to Thomas Muentzer translated by George Williams in *Library of Christian Classics*, Vol. 25 (Philadelphia: Westminster Press, 1957), p. 75.

practice in these churches for many years. Instrumental music was re-introduced only in the face of opposition.[84] The early Anabaptists also soon made much use of singing and produced many original hymns of their own. The first organs were introduced into Mennonite churches in 1764 and 1765. Several conservative branches of these heirs of the sixteenth century Anabaptists have never accepted instrumental music, and it is estimated that about one-third of the Mennonite churches in North America use an instrument.[85]

The very term used in musical circles for unaccompanied singing sums up the evidence of church history. *A cappella* comes from the Latin by way of Italian and means "in the style of the church," "as is done in the church." The classical form of church music is unaccompanied song. To abstain from the use of the instrument is not a peculiar aberration of "a frontier American sect": this was easily, until comparatively recent times, the majority tradition of Christian history. Virtually no one has said it is wrong to worship *a cappella*, whereas many have thought instrumental music in worship is wrong. It may not appear to be true today, but against the whole sweep of Christian history *a cappella* music is the truly ecumenical ground to occupy.

---

[84] See John L. Girardeau, *Instrumental Music in the Public Worship of the Church* (Richmond, Va., 1888).

[85] "Music, Church," *Mennonite Encyclopedia*, Volume III (Scottdale, Pa., 1957), pp. 791-795.

QUESTIONS FOR STUDY

1. Are there any passages referring to playing on an instrument in the worship assembly of the church in the early centuries?

2. Are there any passages describing the singing of Christians in the worship assembly?

3. Are there any passages expressly denying the presence of instrumental music in Christian worship?

4. How did early Christian authors account for the presence of instrumental music in Jewish worship in the Old Testament?

5. Give some of the allegories employed by the church fathers for the various Old Testament instruments.

6. In what circumstances do we find statements favorable to instrumental music by early Christian authors? In what settings do early Christian authors condemn instrumental music?

7. What is the etymology of the word psalm? Did Jews and Christians normally use the word in its etymological sense?

8. Does the meaning of the word psalm say anything about Christian musical practice? To what purpose did early Christian authors put the literal meaning of the word psalm?

9. What is the significance of the historical evidence in determining Christian practice in worship? How may advocates of instrumental music in Christian worship answer the historical argument?

10. Do you find the cultural context of early Christianity a sufficient explanation for its musical practices? What aspects of the Christian attitude were influenced by culture?

11. What religious groups have rejected instrumental music in their worship?

THEOLOGY

Chapter III

DOCTRINAL CONSIDERATIONS

Thus far this study has shown that the circumstances of New Testament times and the testimony of church history point to a negative conclusion concerning the use of instrumental music in early Christian worship. Was there some reason other than cultural or sociological for the absence of instrumental music in early Christian worship? We now turn to the doctrinal or theological aspect of the study. This is the consideration on which the decision about Christian practice today must be made. I would argue that *a cappella* music is more consistent with the nature of Christian worship. It is really the nature of Christian worship which determined early Christian practice and should determine present practice. There are doctrinal considerations which give meaning and significance to the Biblical and historical evidence.

Nature of Worship

Worship is what man offers to God. The important thing in Christian worship is not our uplift, what pleases our senses, or what we find aesthetically satisfying. Instrumental music may put one in a certain mood, may stir his heart, may stimulate high sentiments (as well as lower or lesser sentiments), but one's feelings are not his worship. Instrumental music performed by someone else cannot be something I offer to God. The thesis presented here is that although worship may have aspects which are emotional, aesthetic, and appeal to the senses in a wholesome way, it is not to be determined by these aspects but by what is rational, spiritual, and verbal. Music has rich emotional and aesthetic aspects. What is said in the following pages is not meant to depreciate this, but to place the emphasis in religious music on a more fundamental aspect.

Worship is grounded in man's relation to God, as creature to Creator. That means man must come before God on God's terms. The gifts man offers are those God appoints. Instrumental music was itself an act of worship, and not just an aid, in the Old Testament (2 Chronicles 29:26-29). It was a separate act. Playing an instrument is doing something different, something else from singing. To offer mechanical music acceptably would require an explicit authorization from God in the New Testament.

Spiritual Worship

There is a real question whether the offering of instrumental music is consistent with the spiritual nature of Christian worship. As a mechanical act, producing instrumental music is distinct from the offering of spiritual worship, that is, what comes from the spiritual nature of man. Here Christians should not allow subjective preferences to guide their thinking, but should allow their theology of worship to arise out of New Testament statements about the nature of worship.

Christian worship is to be done "in the spirit" (John 4:24). Vocal expressions are peculiarly well suited to the expression of spiritual worship, to the expressing of what comes from the spirit of man and through the Spirit of God. They are rational, not in the sense of non-emotional, but as proceeding from and appealing to the highest nature of man. The whole self (including the emotions) is involved in Christian worship, but the mind (reason) is to be in control. Instrumental music can express feelings and emotions. Vocal music can express the will and intellect. The latter is better suited for the communion of spirit with Spirit. In vocal music there is an immediate contact. In instrumental music there is an intermediary. The voice is much more a matter of one's self than any other gift of praise can be. Vocal music thus best corresponds to the nature of man's relationship to God.

Christians present their "bodies as a living sacrifice, holy and acceptable to God, which is your spiritual worship"

---

[86] C. F. D. Moule, "Sanctuary and Sacrifice in the Church of the New Testament," *Journal of Theological Studies* I (April, 1950), pp. 34f.

(Romans 12:1). They are "like living stones . . . built into a spiritual house, to be a holy priesthood, to offer spiritual sacrifices acceptable to God through Jesus Christ" (I Peter 2:5). These passages speak of "rational service" (*logikē latreia*) and "spiritual sacrifice" (*pneumatikē thusia*). These expressions are virtually synonymous.[86] The adjective *logikē* was current in the philosophical literature for the distinctive nature of man, the reasoning power (*logos*), which distinguished him from animals, and his spiritual nature in contrast to his sensual nature. In this way *logikē thusia* (rational or spiritual sacrifice) was used of prayers and hymns in contrast to the animal sacrifices of pagan and Jewish cults. In the Hermetic Writings (pagan philosophical-religious works) note the following:

> Accept my reason's offerings pure, from soul and heart stretched up to Thee. (I, 31)
> Sing with me praises all ye Powers! . . .
> Thy Reason sings through me Thy praises. Take back through me the All into Thy Reason—my reasonable oblation!
> Thus cry the Powers in me. They sing Thy praise, Thou All; they do Thy Will . . . .
> To thee, thou Parent of my Bringing into Birth, as unto God I, Tat, send reasonable offerings. O God and Father, thou art the Lord, thou art the Mind. Receive from me oblations reasonable as thou would'st wish. (XIII, 18f., 21)[87]

The thought was extended to silent, intellectual meditation in contrast to any outward expression of worship. There is no indication that the New Testament carried the thought this far, and early Christian writers, as we have seen, disown such a limitation.

The spiritualization of worship as properly belonging to the spiritual or rational (*logikē*) nature also finds expression in interestamental Jewish literature.

> [The angels] offer to the Lord a sweet-smelling savour, a reasonable and bloodless offering. (*Testament of Levi* 3:6)[88]

---

[87]The translation is that of G. R. S. Mead, *Thrice Greatest Hermes* (London, 1964), Vol. II, pp. 12, 145f.

[88]R. H. Charles, *The Apocrypha and Pseudepigrapha of the Old Testament* (Oxford: Clarendon Press, 1913), Vol. II, p. 306. Judaism came to regard prayer and repentance as better than sacrifice.

Patristic literature picked up this characterization of worship. Hesychius of Jerusalem was quite explicit in relating this to vocal praise:

> The church now promises to offer not only the praise which it has in common with the physical creation, but to give glory with song, which is to offer the spiritual and intellectual hymnody. This is to sing to God properly . . . .
> Rational [*logikē*]· praise pleases God more than worship according to the law. (*Fragments on the Psalms* 98:30, 31 in PG 93:1232C)

Similar language is found earlier in Justin's *Dialogue with Trypho* 116-118.

Contemporary usage identified what was *logikē* as belonging to the realm of words or concepts rather than that of matter. The term identified a "spiritual or immaterial system of worship."[89] As was observed above, early Christians saw their prayers and hymns as a more acceptable sacrifice than the offerings of animals. The noun *logos* in Greek meant both reason and word. Worship of such a nature proceeds from the reasoning faculty in man and can be expressed in word. Similarly, what is spiritual corresponds to the spirit in man. Worship characterized in this way can neither proceed from nor appeal to the lower nature of man, but is not thereby simply "intellectual" worship. Moreover, vocal music is something a person produces in and from himself. It is thus the most appropriate expression of the offering of the self to God (Rom. 12:1). Vocal expressions of prayer and hymns are naturally suited for the expression of worship which comes from this highest nature of man.

Edification

When Paul was confronted with disorders in the worship assembly of the church at Corinth, he invoked the standard of "what edifies the church" to govern the conduct of the worshippers (I Cor. 14:4, 6, 9, 12, 19, 26). The true language of worship is not just directed to God but also serves for mutual help. The purpose of coming together, and not simply offering one's worship alone, is that edification in Christ can occur. Therefore, what goes on in the assembly must be

---

[89]Moule, *loc. cit.*

intelligible, understandable. One may note the emphasis which Paul gives to the mind (understanding—1 Corinthians 14:15, 19). This is a principle which ties edification to the "rational" nature of worship. Ephesians 5:19 and Colossians 3:16 have not only the praise "to God" but the speaking to "one another" dimension. Accordingly "teaching and admonishing" have a place in Christian worship. Singing is such a communal act and provides for mutual edification.

Edification for Paul in I Corinthians 14 meant intelligible, verbal instruction, in contrast to speaking in unintelligible (to those present) tongues (vs. 19). No one is edified by mere sound. It is in this context that he makes disparaging reference to instruments of music ("lifeless" or "soulless" things—verses 7, 8; cf. 13:1). The foreign language would be comparable to an uncertain sound by instruments. By way of contrast, rational, spiritual, vocal music corresponds to Paul's criterion. "Each one has a hymn, a lesson, a revelation, a tongue, or an interpretation. Let all things be done for edification" (I Cor. 14:26). The synagogue emphasized teaching and did not have instrumental music. The temple emphasized ritual, and it did have instrumental music. Further, in Christian history, where edification has been central, instrumental music has been in the background, but where ritual has been in the forefront, then the instrument has been prominent. An obvious contrast is between the Calvinist churches of the Reformation and the Catholic Church of the late Middle Ages.

It is difficult to conceive of instrumental music contributing to the Biblical meaning of edification, building one up in the faith. It is more likely to interfere with the purposes of edification than to contribute to them. Since worship is a corporate act of the assembled congregation of believers, the opportunity should be given for all to participate in the service of song.

The Classical Form of Church Music

The type of vocal praise evolved in the synagogue and the early church made instrumental music irrelevant. It is only the instrumentally conceived music of modern times that makes us think differently. To reintroduce instrumental music is to take a backward step as regards the spirit of

Christian worship. It is, therefore, no wonder that historians and interpreters of church music agree that *a cappella* singing is the purest and highest type of church music. Many quotations could be assembled on this theme, of which a few are offered here. The authors may not agree on an exclusive stand, but they do agree that this is the classical form of church music.

J. Gelineau, *Voices and Instruments in Christian Worship*,[90] is an important study by a Roman Catholic. Although he defends a place for instrumental accompaniment, he testifies to the priority of vocal music in the Catholic tradition.

> Pius X, before discussing instrumental music, recalls that "the music proper to the Church is purely vocal music." (p. 148)
> Nevertheless the abundance and clearness of the texts in which the Fathers of the Church have discussed the question can leave us in no doubt about the content and firmness of their teaching: musical instruments are to be excluded from the worship of the New Alliance. (pp. 150f.)
> Never can the vocal and spiritual praise of the Word of God be supplied or supplanted, in worship in spirit and in truth, by the sound of musical instruments alone. (pp. 151f.)
> The fundamental principle: vocal praise alone is essential to Christian worship. Instruments are only accessory. (pp. 155f.)

K. G. Fellerer speaks in the same vein:

> The "worship in spirit" (Jn. 4:23), with its implied rejection of a purely esthetic enjoyment of music, was the basis for the general repudiation of instrumental music, customary in pagan worship . . . .
> The basis of Christian ecclesiastical music was its vocal character. It was the prayer of the community sung by the people.[91]

---

[90] London: Burns & Oates, 1964.

[91] *History of Catholic Church Music* (Baltimore: Helicon Press, 1961), p. 13.

Edward Dickinson's Music in the History of the Western Church[92] is an important testimony:

> In rejecting the support of instruments and developing for the first time an exclusively vocal art, and in breaking loose from the restrictions of antique metre which in Greek and Greco-Roman music had forced melody to keep step with strict prosodic measure, Christian music parted company with pagan art, threw the burden of expression not, like Greek music, upon rhythm, but upon melody, and found in this absolute vocal melody a new art principle of which all the worship music of modern Christendom is the natural fruit. More vital still than these special forms and principles, comprehending and necessitating them, was the true ideal of music, proclaimed once for all by the fathers of the liturgy. This ideal is found in the distinction of the church style from the secular style, the expression of the universal mood of prayer, rather than the expression of individual, fluctuating, passionate emotion with which secular music deals . . . .

The originality of which Dickinson speaks probably belongs to Judaism, and so his statement needs modifications in points, but he has the right feeling for the distinctive character of Christian religious expression. Finally, note the following from Luther D. Reed:

> The great bulk of church music, historically considered, is vocal. Plain song developed without thought of instruments, and in our use of it today organ accompaniment should be kept quite subordinate. The congregational chorale was originally accompanied by the choir; and even now the organ accompaniment should support and bring out the melody and not suppress it. The older polyphonic compositions for the choir—on whose extent and value we have said many musicians today are learning—were entirely vocal. Emil Nauman says that "the great works of the great masters of sacred music . . . would never have been called into existence had their authors been limited to an organ accompaniment."
>
> More important than considerations of history are the qualities of purity and distinctiveness which characterize good vocal music. The organ and orchestra produce mechanical effects. Vocal music of

---

[92] New York: Scribner's, 1902, pp. 68f.

quality has a tonal purity that is unique. Even Richard Wagner, who appreciated and developed the modern orchestra in connection with his great musical dramas, said, "The human voice is the immediate organ for delivering the sacred text . . . . If church music is ever to be restored to its original purity, vocal music must oust the instrumental and occupy the place this has usurped."[93]

In making this plea for unaccompanied vocal singing in church I should not be understood as saying that just because the singing is unaccompanied it measures up to the standards of Christian worship—as edifying, spiritual, and an appropriate offering of man to God. I am simply saying that vocal music is best fitted to express the nature of Christian worship. And this is also the recognition of theorists of church music.

The Christian desires to offer his best to God and so will be concerned with developing the best types of vocal music and rendering it to the best of his ability. The musical aspects of the singing serve to reinforce the vocal content and so to deepen the impression of the words, hold the attention, add an emotional impact to the ideas, and elevate the thoughts. The rhythm and melody serve as an aid to the vocal element in achieving the purposes of spiritual worship and edification. The specific forms of rhythm and melody will be in accord with the types of music native to the people who are worshipping—whether Western, Oriental,African, or whatever. These culturally conditioned forms are to be governed by the standards of spiritual, edifying worship and must be designed to express the true nature of Christian worship. Aesthetic considerations have their place and will vary from culture to culture but must be subordinated to other considerations in Christian worship. Aesthetic abuses can be present in vocal music as well as instrumental, but instrumental music is more likely to interfere with the standards here set up than is vocal music.

Conclusion

There are good historical, theological, and musicological

---

[93] *Worship* (Philadelphia: Muhlenberg Press, 1959), p. 183.

grounds to engage only in *a cappella* music in public worship. This is safe, ecumenical ground that all can agree is acceptable. Instrumental music cannot be confirmed as authorized in the text of the New Testament. It did not exist in Christian worship for centuries after the New Testament. Vocal music is more consistent with the nature of Christian worship. Instrumental music in comparison to vocal music (as incense in comparison to prayer) is, as the church fathers said, a falling back to a lower level (the Old Testament level) of religious expression. It introduces into man's relationship to God an act lacking specific apostolic authorization.

This study is not offered in a judgmental spirit toward those who use instrumental music in worship. Rather it has sought to be an objective piece of historical research, and a statement of the theological reasons which seem to give meaning to this history. Although the author has tried to be cautious in drawing conclusions, he does hope to have demonstrated that only *a cappella* music in the public worship of the church rests on good Biblical, historical, and theological grounds.

QUESTIONS FOR STUDY

1. How does the nature of God determine the nature of worship?

2. How does the New Testament describe the nature of worship?

3. What did the terms "rational worship" and "spiritual sacrifice" mean in the context of their time? What implications does this have for the question of instrumental music?

4. What criterion for "what is done in the assembly" does Paul appeal to in 1 Corinthians 14? Does this have any significance for the kind of music used in the assembly?

5. Is instrumental music an aid to worship or an act of worship?

6. Can something mechanical be a part of spiritual worship? Consider acts other than playing on an instrument in giving an answer.

7. What is the role of the emotions in spiritual worship?

8. What is the relation of the voice to the intellectual and spiritual nature of man? Do you think the voice is more suitable than other means for expressing spiritual worship?

9. What is meant by the expression "the classical form of church music"?

10. What should be the relations between brethren who differ on the subject of instrumental music?

ANCIENT AUTHORS AND WORKS CITED

Acts of John—Second century apocryphal writing.

Acts of Thomas—Third century apocryphal writing.

Ambrose—Bishop of Milan, 374-397, and one of the most influential of the Latin bishops of his day.

Apostolic Constitutions—A compilation of ecclesiastical regulations made in the late fourth century from earlier sources.

Aristides—Greek orator of the second century A.D.

Arnobius—Convert to Christianity from North Africa, who died about 330.

Athanasius—Bishop of Alexandria from 328 to 373 and champion of theological orthodoxy. One of the most important men in the fourth century church.

Athenagoras—Second century Greek apologist for Christianity.

Augustine—Bishop of Hippo in North Africa from 395 to 430 and the most significant formative influence on the thought of Latin Christendom after his time.

Basil of Caesarea—Known as "the Great." Bishop of Caesarea in Cappadocia from 370 to 379 and the most influential Greek bishop of his time.

Canons of Basil—Collection of ecclesiastical regulations from the late fourth century, probably without any connection with Basil.

Chrysostom—John the "Golden-mouth." Was presbyter at Antioch (386-398) and bishop of Constantinople (398-404). The greatest preacher of the ancient Greek church and in general a reliable guide to the meaning of New Testament words.

Clement of Alexandria—Philosophically minded Christian author who gives much information on customs of his time. Died about A.D. 215.

Cyril of Jerusalem—Bishop of Jerusalem from about 349 to 386.

Ephraim Syrus—The classic author of Syriac speaking Christianity. Lived 307-373.

Eusebius of Caesarea—Bishop and church historian. The principal source for early Christian history up to the fourth century.

Gregory of Nazianzus—Lived from 329 to 389. A great orator and champion of orthodoxy.

Gregory of Nyssa—Lived from about 330 to 395. Brother of Basil the Great, and a philosophical theologian.

Hermetic Writings—Pagan philosophical and religious writings from Egypt, written during the early Christian centuries, and deriving their name from Hermes, the Greek messenger of the gods.

Hesychius of Jerusalem—Fifth century Greek Christian author.

Hilary of Poitiers—Bishop of Poitiers in France from about 353 to 367. An important defender of orthodoxy.

Hippolytus—Greek Christian author who lived in Rome in the early third century.

Ignatius of Antioch—Bishop of Antioch at the beginning of the second century who wrote seven letters to churches in Asia Minor and Rome.

Isidore of Pelusium—Abbot of a monastery near the mouth of the Nile. Died about A.D. 450.

Jerome—Latin Bible scholar and translator, who lived 342 to 420.

Josephus—Jewish historian (about A.D. 37 to after 100) who sought to commend Roman rule to the Jews and Judaism to the people of the Roman empire.

Judith—A Jewish apocryphal book written probably in the second century B.C.

Justin Martyr—Defender of Christianity and most important Christian author from the mid-second century.

Lucian of Samosata—A Greek author of the second century A.D. from Syria.

Methodius—Christian bishop of Olympus in Lycia. Died about 311.

Niceta—Bishop of Remesiana in what is now Yugoslavia, who died about 414.

Odes of Solomon—Collection of Christian hymns in the early second century.

Origen—Christian teacher at Alexandria and then Caesarea, who lived from about 185 to 254. The greatest thinker and most prolific Christian author of the early centuries, most of whose works have not survived in the original Greek.

Philo—An Alexandrian Jewish philosopher (about 20 B.C. to A.D. 50) whose writings are a major source of information for Hellenistic Judaism and Greek philosophy in the first century.

Philostratus—Pagan author of the early third century.

Psalms of Solomon—A first century B.C. collection of Jewish hymns.

Pseudo-Clementines—Writings falsely claiming to come from Clement of Rome, containing early Jewish Christian views and then reworked in the interests of orthodoxy, in their present form from the fourth century.

Second Clement—Christian sermon from the middle of the second century.

Sibylline Oracles—Originally pagan prophetic writings which were later imitated by Jews and then by Christians in order to promote their beliefs in the pagan world.

Sirach—At the beginning of the second century B.C. Jesus ben Sira wrote this work, belonging to Jewish wisdom literature and which is sometimes called Ecclesiasticus.

Synesius of Cyrene—Bishop of Ptolemais, 410 to 414, who remained more Greek than Christian in his thought.

Tatian—Defender of Christianity against Greek culture in the second-half of the second century.

Tertullian—The most extensive Christian writer in Latin before the fourth century. Lived in Carthage from about 160 to 220.

Testament of Job—A pseudepigraphal writing of uncertain date and origin.

Theodoret—Bishop of Cyrrhus in Syria, 423-458, and a leading exponent of the Antiochian school of interpretation.

Vision of Paul—Fourth century apocryphal writing.

GLOSSARY

Apocrypha—The technical term employed by Protestants for the writings included in the Roman Catholic Old Testament but not included in the Hebrew Old Testament and not accepted by Jews and Protestants as part of the Old Testament canon.

Classical—The normative period of a language, as for Greek the period especially from 500 to 330 B.C.

Dead Sea Scrolls—The Jewish writings produced from the third century B.C. to the first century A.D. by the Qumran community on the Northwest shore of the Dead Sea and hidden in caves in that region during the Jewish revolt against Rome in A.D. 66-70.

Essenes—A Jewish sect in the first century who are generally held to be the group which produced the Dead Sea Scrolls.

Etymology—The origin of a word, its root meaning.

Hellenistic—Pertaining to the Greek culture which permeated the area around the Mediterranean Sea following the conquests of Alexander the Great.

Intertestamental—The period between the Old and the New Testaments; some of the writings called intertestamental are not strictly so but were contemporary with the New Testament and early Christianity.

Lexicon—A dictionary of word meanings and uses.

Midrash—Jewish commentaries on Old Testament materials.

Mishna—The codification of Jewish legal material compiled by Rabbi Judah at the end of the second century A.D.

Old Latin Translation—The translation of the Bible into Latin, parts of which (at least) were made in the second century and which was revised by Jerome at the end of the fourth century to produce the Vulgate.

Orthodoxy—Normative correctness in Christian thought. Literally, "that which seems right."

Oxyrhynchus papyri—The writings on papyrus material found in Egypt at the town of this name.

Pseudepigrapha—Spurious writings falsely claiming a religious authority which was not theirs, but many of which had a wide circulation among Jews and early Christians.

Rabbinic—Pertaining to the official Jewish teachers who (for the purposes of this study) flourished in the first five centuries of the Christian era.

Septuagint—The Greek translation of the Old Testament begun in the third century B.C.

Talmud—The commentary on the Mishna, sometimes incorporating early material, compiled about the fifth century A.D.

Therapeutae—Jewish sect in Egypt described by Philo and which is usually related to the Essenes.

Ferguson

A Capella Music in the Public Worship...

DEMCO